CW00952697

MADONNA

MADONNA
The Biography

Robert Matthew-Walker

SIDGWICK & JACKSON
LONDON

All photographs courtesy of
London Features International

First published in Great Britain in 1989 by
Sidgwick & Jackson Limited
1 Tavistock Chambers, Bloomsbury Way
London WC1A 2SG

ISBN 0-283-99805-9

Typeset by Hewer Text Composition Services, Edinburgh
Printed in Great Britain by Billing & Sons Ltd, Worcester

"For Joanne Walker"

CONTENTS

INTRODUCTION

When the teen-aged Madonna Ciccone first arrived in New York City in the middle of summer 1976, carrying thirty-five dollars in the pocket of her winter coat, she was embarking on a course which would make her – less than a dozen years later – the most successful and sought-after female singer the world has ever seen.

But she is much more than the woman who has sold in excess of 85 million albums worldwide, more than any other female singer. Madonna is an accomplished and talented actress, on Broadway and in motion pictures. She has become a media phenomenon of such compelling dynamism – a style-setter of world impact – that the giant Pepsi-Cola Corporation paid her around five million dollars to appear in a transworld television ad to promote their drink. Even this hitherto harmless medium was turned into a major international incident through the simultaneous release of a video of the song featured in the ad. Such is her impact that the furore created by the video led Pepsi-Cola to withdraw its sponsorship of her forthcoming world tour – the first time in advertising history that such a thing had happened.

Those years have marked an astonishing journey for Madonna. Her dirt-poor semi-squat in lower Manhattan, where she scavenged in trash-cans for thrown-away French fries and burgers, with prostitutes, drug-abusers and vermin sharing the block, would have destroyed a less determined character. Ten years later, she owns a three-million-dollar Manhattan apartment overlooking Central Park, a Malibu beach house and a personal fortune conservatively reputed to be not less than sixty million dollars.

By any standards, hers is an exceptional story but the rags to riches element is not unique. Many stories can be told, and books written, about people who have 'made it' financially. What sets Madonna apart, what makes her achievement so utterly confounding, is a

1

prodigious combination of sheer and unremitting work, marked by a fierce determination to succeed – but not at any price – and by her multi-faceted talent. One or more of these qualities might just possibly have got her a measure of success, but not consistently so. Her success would have been, as she herself described it, like that of 'a one-act Disco Dolly who was just going to pop in and pop out'.

Nor was she an overnight success: that took five years of hard work, but once she was there she was absolutely determined that she would stay. Madonna somehow always knew, instinctively, that she was destined for lasting fame, even though she has been written off more times than a Formula 1 stock-car. Towards the end of 1988 some self-appointed taste-makers of popular art had begun airily to speak of her in the past tense, a faded has-been, a burned-out 1980s phenomenon of no contemporary interest. Three months later, two years after her previous album, *Like A Prayer* shot straight in at the very top of the pop charts. Suddenly Madonna was on everyone's lips, including those of the commentators who had so recently dismissed her and were now forced to revise their opinion through the new aspects of her creative character revealed for the first time in the new album.

She herself says, 'slowly, as the years go by I've been showing a little bit more of myself. One facet and then another facet. And every time they think they have me understood, I do something else . . . I'm just going to have to work very hard . . . That's the way it works. That's the way it has always worked.'

True enough, but talent and determination do not always go hand in hand. There are many gifted people who are lazy, and who squander their gifts. But in Madonna's case, the deep vein of Catholicism from which she has sprung has undoubtedly sustained her, even in her blackest moments of despair and disappointment. Perhaps she remembers the parable of the talents: Madonna's latest act of contrition has enabled her to come full circle. She has dedicated her newest album to the memory of her mother, the woman who gave Madonna birth to begin her astonishing and fascinating journey – a journey from nowhere to unprecedented world fame. Madonna's story is itself a parable for our age – her success, and the way it has come about, could have happened at no other time.

1

LITTLE NONNI

Towards the end of the second week of August 1958, a casual observer of the television news in the USA could have been forgiven for thinking that only two subjects were of national importance: the scandal surrounding the President's Assistant, Governor Sherman Adams, and the health of Mrs Gladys Presley, mother of Elvis.

Governor Adams had held his post since 1953, but the revelation that he had been the beneficiary of indirect payments in kind, of which the President had always regarded him as being innocent, had blown up into rather more than a storm in a teacup. So much so, in fact, that within a few weeks the ascerbic Governor was forced to resign his office, taking with him a specially inscribed presentation silver bowl, the personal gift of President Dwight D. Eisenhower. This domestic worry was the last thing the President would have wished: the international political scene was troubled by events in the Middle East and by relations with the Communist bloc. The Nationalist government in Taiwan was calling for armed American intervention following the Chinese mainland bombardment of the off-shore islands, Quemoy and Matsu, and the American invasion of Lebanon some weeks earlier.

For Gladys Presley, seriously ill with hepatitis in the Memphis Methodist Hospital to which she had been admitted in July, the arrival at her bedside of her only surviving son, Elvis, on compassionate leave from the US Army, proved to be their last meeting. The course of the final stages of the disease proved inexorable, and early in the morning of 14 August she suffered a fatal heart attack.

The international military obligations of the United States were at that time considerable: Elvis Presley was in the Army as a conscript,

3

required by law to serve as a soldier for two years, and within a few weeks of his mother's death he was posted to Germany, where he remained until his demobilization in 1960.

On the eve of Gladys Presley's death, addressing the General Assembly of the United Nations in New York, President Eisenhower spoke of his beliefs:

> The world that is being remade on this planet . . . is not going to be controlled by any one power or group . . . this world is not going to be committed to any one ideology . . . the dream of world conformity is an impossible dream. . . .

His sentiments were not necessarily original; and they were certainly echoed by his successor, the Democratic President John F. Kennedy, in his inaugural address in January 1961. But what Eisenhower said on 13 August 1958 looked forward to the kind of world which the adult career of a girl born three days after his speech would personify to a dramatic degree.

Madonna Louise Ciccone, named after her mother, was born in the residential village of Rochester, in Oakland county, which is situated in the south-eastern part of the state of Michigan. Rochester is about twenty-five miles north of the state's largest city, Detroit, and, like most of that part of the southern peninsula, its economy is comprised of manufacturing industries and, to a lesser degree, farming. The industrial products are tools, steel components and machinery, spin-offs from the automobile industry which dominates the economy of Detroit, known equally as Motown (Motor-town), and which in turn grew from the important carriage trade established there and in Pontiac in the 1870s by immigrant entrepreneurs.

Being close to Canada, there has always been a fairly strong French community within that part of Michigan, and with it a notable Catholic contingent. The geography today reflects the industrialization of the region: once covered with great woodlands, the timber boom of one hundred years ago has reduced the trees to the merest fraction of their previous acreage. Modern farms have created much wealth, and the climate benefits from a long growing season, tempered by the proximity of Lakes Erie and Michigan which are respectively to the east and west of the southern Michigan peninsula. Rochester is a pleasant town which, when Madonna Ciccone was born, had a population of about six-and-a-half thousand people.

The Ciccones originally came from Pacentro, a small village near Aquila (or L'Aquila degli Abruzzi, to give it the full name), the capital of the Abruzzi province in central Italy. Aquila is situated on the Pescara river, about sixty miles north-east of Rome. Madonna Ciccone's great-grandfather, Nicola Pietro Ciccone, always called Pietro, was born in Pacentro in 1867, and grew to a tall, handsome and well-built man, according to his daughter-in-law's sister, Bambina di Julio. Pietro was barely able to read or write, however, and following his marriage in 1883 to a beautiful young girl, Anna Maria Mancini, he insisted that their children, including their son Gaetano, obtain a decent education. But as a young man Gaetano found that his schooling counted for little in terms of finding suitable work in Pacentro. Shortly before the end of World War I, there were few prospects for him in the village, and he asked the local priest to write to his brother, who was a foundry worker in Pittsburgh, Pennsylvania, to enlist his help in finding a job in America.

After a little while, employment was found for him, and at the age of sixteen Gaetano went to America by himself, telling his fifteen-year-old girlfriend Michelina that he would come back to Pacentro one day to marry her, and that they would go to America as man and wife. Gaetano was as good as his word: on his return, he and Michelina were married on 21 December 1919 in the parish church of Pacentro. He was eighteen and Michelina seventeen. A few weeks later they both went to Pittsburgh, where Gaetano had found a house and a job in a large steel-works. Their first child, Mario, was born the following year, and their sixth and last son, Silvio (Madonna's father, who was always known as 'Tony'), was born in 1934.

There was plenty of work available in the steel industry in Pittsburgh, especially during and after World War II, but by the time he left school, Tony Ciccone had other ideas: he clearly possessed considerable character and determination. Anxious to break free, he managed to go to college and obtain an engineering degree and then, following his graduation, Tony was called up to do his national service in the Air Force.

One of Tony's best friends from the Air Force invited him home to Bay City, Michigan, for a few days and it was there that he met Madonna Veronica, the eldest daughter of the house. It was love at first sight for Tony and Madonna; following his demobilization, and with his diploma, he was now more readily able to seek his own fortune outside of the environs of Pittsburgh. Tony and Madonna were married within a few weeks of his leaving the Air Force. From his parent's home in Pittsburgh, the twenty-one-year-old Tony Ciccone crossed Lake Erie and the state line to settle with his new bride in Rochester, Michigan, drawn to the tool and machinery manufacturing industries of the southern peninsula.

With his professional qualifications and his natural intelligence and energy, Tony soon found himself a well-paid job with the Chrysler Corporation, and within a short while he had become a highly regarded member of his firm's staff. It's just as well that Tony had a good salary because his wife gave birth to six children altogether, the first five appearing at yearly intervals after their marriage. The first, a boy born in 1956, was christened Anthony after his father; his brother Martin followed in 1957, and Madonna Louise, born on 16 August 1958, was Tony and Madonna's first daughter. A sister for Madonna, named Paula, was born in 1959, and a third boy, Christopher, appeared in 1960. Five children under the age of five would be a handful for any mother, but Tony's wife revelled in her motherhood and regarded herself as extremely fortunate. She also had the advantage of occasional domestic help. Their family was completed by the birth in 1962 of their third daughter Melanie.

Tony was determined that his children should have a strict Catholic upbringing, as he himself had had. Like most first-generation Italian-American families, they adhered to the traditional religious and ethical beliefs, but the remarkable thing about the Ciccone children is that as adults they all get on with each other extremely well, and look back on their early childhood with affection. Later in life, Madonna would speak admiringly of her father's strength and integrity, and all the children recall the loving atmosphere at home in their early years.

As the first daughter, Madonna was the apple of her father's eye, but it is clear that she was never spoilt by Tony. Her earliest memories are of her mother's indulgence for her; at night, waking up in the small hours, Madonna would go to her parents' bedroom and stand at the door for a while, watching them sleep, before she would climb over their bed and snuggle down between them, close up to her mother's beautiful silky-red nightgown. Tony would not be too pleased at this virtual nightly interruption of his sleep; perhaps he felt that his other children might resent 'Little Nonni', as she was affectionately nicknamed in the family, sharing their parents' bed, but her mother always allowed her to stay.

Disaster struck in 1962, soon after the birth of Melanie, when Tony was alarmed to learn of his wife's concern over her health. Breast cancer was diagnosed, at a time when early screening for the condition was extremely rare and treatments were not very successful. Madonna Senior bore her affliction with a calm fatalism, secured by a profound faith, and managed to keep going, hiding her condition and fears from her children as best she could; but her growing physical weakness could not be concealed for ever. She would sit on the couch with her children but she could not play with them. 'Little Nonni' did not understand why, and resented her mother's unwillingness to play. On one occasion, the girl climbed on her mother's back and began hitting her: it was only when this childish tantrum reduced her mother to tears that she realized something was wrong. It was a profound realization for 'Nonni'; up till then, she had thought that the world was hers, a private stomping-ground from which she could take any opportunity. Now she knew, at a very early age, that life was not predestined to be forever good, trouble-free, and limitless.

Not long after this incident, her mother had to be admitted to hospital where she remained, intermittently, for almost a year. During this period, the members of the Ciccone family, previously so lively and out-going, were stricken with uncertainty and worry. 'Nonni' would sometimes see her father alone, crying, inconsolable. She and her brothers and sisters were cared for on a daily basis by several housekeepers, and would stay, one or two at a time, in the homes of aunts and uncles in Bay City, where their grandmother also did all that she could to provide motherly care. But it was not and never could be the same.

Tony took his children to visit their mother in hospital, and she made an effort to laugh and joke with them, playing down the seriousness of her illness. Madonna still did not realize how desperate the situation was when, one day, her mother asked her for a hamburger. By this stage the invalid was unable to take much

7

food. Madonna thought the request was ludicrous and shrieked with laughter but, as it turned out, it was the last thing she was to be able to do for her mother. Early in 1965, with 'Nonni' now a precocious six-year-old, her mother finally died and Tony and his six children became, in the phrase of a later generation, a one-parent family.

As a devout Catholic, Tony turned to religion for strength at this tragic time: his children all went to Catholic schools, and were made to attend Mass every morning before school lessons began. He hired a succession of full-time housekeepers to try to cope with his lively brood while he carried on working to support them all, but perhaps in some kind of reaction to their mother's death, they were quite wild at this stage and a handful for anyone to deal with. Madonna was a bit of a tomboy, who enjoyed playing with her older brothers, but she was also deeply religious in her child-like way. Her older brother Martin recalls one occasion when he owed his life to her beliefs. He was seven years old when he managed to climb a seventy-foot-high electrical tower in Rochester; near the top, he became alarmed and could not get down. Madonna was with him and, seeing his predicament, quickly climbed up after him and handed her brother a crucifix which their mother had given her. She told him to put it on and only by wearing it would he get down safely. He did as he was told and, without a second thought, followed his sister down the tower to the ground. Madonna's faith made a big impression on him, and after that he was somewhat in awe of her self-assured and confident attitude to life and religion. For the young Madonna, however, what she did for her brother was the most natural thing in the world; she was a member of the local Brownie pack and no stranger to climbing.

In the end, the children proved too much for any housekeeper to deal with so some of them, including Madonna, were sent to stay with their maternal grandmother in Bay City, ninety miles to the north of Rochester on the Michigan Railroad. The loving attentions of her grandmother, who spoilt her to a degree she had never before experienced, went some way towards healing Madonna's hurt and uncertainty at the death of her mother. She was allowed to stay out late in the evenings with other children in the neighbourhood; she was cosseted and made much more of an individual fuss of than at home. After the shock of her mother's death, she formed a very strong attachment to the 'mother figure' her grandmother had temporarily become: they had both lost a loved one, and were naturally drawn closer as a result.

'When I was growing up, I loved my granny. She wasn't as strict as my parents, so I loved to stay with her. We could have twelve desserts at her place and stay out after ten. Boys were my main interest and she let me go out with them when I wanted and even drink bottles of beer. She wasn't like my folks. They minded if I did one little thing, like wear lip-gloss or opaque panty-hose. I don't mean nylon stockings that you could see through, or anything sheer. Just tights, that's all. I didn't understand them.'

Bay City, as its name suggests, is a port of entry for the southern peninsula of Michigan. It is situated on the mouth of the Saginaw River where it joins Saginaw Bay, an inlet of Lake Huron. It is a rich city, made so by a regular shipping trade in farm produce and industrial products. Like most ports, it has a lively nightlife and it is also rich in historical associations, notably Red Indian. It must have seemed a vibrant and wonderful place to the little six-year-old girl from Rochester.

Gradually it was sister Paula who took over the role of the family tomboy, as Madonna began to discover certain methods of getting others to comply with her wishes, principally by turning on the charm, or what she would later term 'feminine wiles'. She was becoming adept at wrapping her father round her little finger but these tricks did not go down too well with her older brothers, who would sometimes hang her up by her knickers on the clothesline if she seemed to get above herself.

Tony had insisted that all the children should take piano lessons every week but after a year of lessons Madonna didn't take to the instrument and decided that she had had enough. Using her charm, she managed to persuade her father to let her take dance classes instead. She was enrolled in a class which taught not only ballet, but also tap, jazz and baton twirling, and she took to it immediately. Madonna remembers loving to dance at this age: 'When I was a little girl, I used to turn on the record player and dance in the basement by myself, and sometimes I gave dance lessons to my girlfriends.'

She continues, 'As I got older I started giving dance lessons to boys too. The first guy I gave lessons to, the song was "Honky Tonk Women" by the Rolling Stones . . . it was really sexy.'

At first she listened to Johnny Mathis, Harry Belafonte and

9

Sam Cooke, and her tastes moved towards pop music later on. 'I moved into things like "The Letter" by The Box Tops and The Archies' "Sugar, Sugar" (I *loved* that record) and "Incense and Peppermints" by Strawberry Alarm Clock and "Quinn the Eskimo" [a Bob Dylan ditty called "The Mighty Quinn"].'

There was another very important style of music currently emerging right on her doorstep. In 1960, the thirty-year-old black songwriter Berry Gordy Junior formed a new record label called Tamla Motown. It concentrated solely upon black American singers and did not, at first, exhibit any distinctive musical traits. By the mid 1960s, however, the characteristic Motown sound had become fully developed, and the label, coinciding with the rise of the black consciousness movement in the USA and the winning of great advances in civil rights did much to desegregate black music (or what used to be called 'race music') throughout the world. Young Madonna Ciccone, with her greater personal freedom in Bay City, and with her natural musical gifts now beginning to manifest themselves, was keen on Motown, especially the girl groups.

'We lived in a real integrated neighbourhood . . . and all the kids had Motown and black stuff. And they had yard dances in their back yards, little 45 turntables and a stack of records, and everyone just danced in the driveway and in the yard. I really liked The Shirelles, The Ronettes, Martha Reeves and the Vandellas and The Supremes.' Early in 1966, Madonna had been entranced by Nancy Sinatra's worldwide hit 'These Boots Are Made For Walkin'' and by the singer's appearance, with her 'go-go boots, mini-skirt, blonde hair and fake eyelashes'. She also liked Chubby Checker's 'Twist', to which she would do the limbo in the back yard.

However young Madonna was, the ferment of America in the 1960s could not have failed to have some effect on her, changing as it did the beliefs, hopes and dreams of all the generations that lived through the decade. On 22 November 1963, in Dallas, Texas, President John F. Kennedy was assassinated: this shocking event transformed the world. His epousement of the black civil rights movement, and his brother Robert's determination as Attorney General to smash organized crime, signalled an administration devoted to change. Such change matched the spirit of the times, at least among the youth of the world, but found violent reactionary forces ranged against it. The Quemoy and Matsu Islands are about as far from mainland China as Long Island is from mainland USA but President Eisenhower's support for the Nationalists at the time of Madonna's birth has now been shown to have been the spark which led China to support the North Vietnamese incursions into the South. Of course, it was the South Vietnamese government that enjoyed the deeply committed support of the anti-Communist United States. The Vietnam War, in which at one time the USA had over 500,000 soldiers on active duty, stretched the fabric of American society to the limit and occasionally beyond it. At home there was an explosion of political protest, fed by the Vietnam War and also by black consciousness movements. Rock music erupted onto the scene, led by British groups, headed by the Beatles, and fed by the coming age of the 'Baby Boom' generation (those born during the years 1945-50), allied to a sexual freedom made easy by more liberal laws and the availability of the Pill. More of America's enlightened leaders were assassinated: Dr Martin Luther King Jr, Robert Kennedy and the Black Panther leader, Malcolm X. All of these things combined to produce a collective culture-shock which ran counter to the established standards of older generations and made it acceptable, almost obligatory, for the young to rebel against their peers.

In 1967 when Tony Ciccone announced to his children that he was to remarry, the bride being one of their housemaids Joan, it was not news that was greeted with universal joy. The major positive result was that the family were reunited at their Rochester home, with their father and a new stepmother. But the children, split up and subjected to various outside influences and having also had to endure a succession of unsatisfactory housekeepers as Tony strove to keep the family together, had clearly adored their natural mother and were not quick to adjust to a new female head of the household. Perhaps the transition was most difficult for the eldest daughter, Madonna, who had been named after her mother, had crept into her parents' bed at night, and who had previously felt that she was her father's favourite.

Equally, for Joan, the prospect of taking on six young children could not have been an easy one to contemplate. Madonna herself, when asked about her relationship with Joan, has always resisted answering the questions but it is obvious that she found the change difficult to come to terms with. Her stepmother was, as Madonna

11

has said, 'really gung-ho, very strict, and it was hard to accept her as an authority figure and the new number one female in my father's life. He wanted us to call her Mom, not her first name.' This was a mistake, but a natural one, by Tony. Madonna remembers it being 'really hard to get the word "Mother" out of my mouth. It was really painful.' And yet, as she has also admitted with admirable frankness, she had earlier morbidly wanted to 'find out my parents weren't my real parents, so I could be an orphan and feel sorry for myself, or I wanted everyone to die in a car accident so I wouldn't have parents to tell me what to do.'

As the oldest girl, and with a stepsister Jennifer being born in 1968 and a stepbrother Mario the following year, she found herself being required to take on responsibilities which were new to her. Had her mother lived and given birth to two more children, it is likely that Madonna would have been asked to help more with the chores anyway but as she grew into her teens, she began to resent the 'little mother' role she was now frequently asked to perform. 'I felt like all of my adolescence was spent taking care of babies and changing diapers and baby-sitting. I have to say I resented it, because when everybody was out playing, I was stuck with all these adult responsibilities.'

The responsibilities must have been even more difficult to shoulder after the glamour and freedom of her life in Bay City and the stimulating influences she had encountered there. Several of her uncles, themselves only a few years older than Anthony and Martin, had formed a rock band and this was a world that was very attractive to Madonna. She had also become addicted to the cinema and was enchanted in particular by the colour, music and drama of movies from the 1930s and 1940s. 'I really loved them because they allowed you to fantasize. I'd watch them and think about what I wanted to be when I grew up.' Among her favourite stars were Carole Lombard and Judy Holliday, Marilyn Monroe (she describes her as 'my first movie idol'), Brigitte Bardot and Grace Kelly. 'They were all just incredibly funny and they were silly and sweet. I saw myself in them, my funniness and my need to boss people around, and at the same time to be taken care of. My knowingness and my innocence both.'

By any standards, 1968 was a watershed in international affairs: the uprisings in Czechoslovakia, the Paris riots and strikes, the

Tet offensive and battle for Hue in Vietnam, the melodrama of that year's American presidential election which culminated in the resurgence of Richard Nixon – few remained untouched by such events. For the Ciccones, 1968 brought more personal tragedies. Michelina, who as a dewy-eyed seventeen-year-old had emigrated to America with Gaetano in 1920, died; some months later, Gaetano himself succumbed to a heart attack. With both of his beloved parents dead, and with a new wife and new children, Tony's preoccupations were more and more directed towards his own family.

Tony viewed Madonna's growing independence with a mixture of indulgence and sternness. She was still deeply religious, and until she was eleven or twelve years old, she believed the devil lived in the basement of their house and she would run as fast as possible up the stairs to escape his clutches (shades of nightmares on Elm Street!). For several years she wanted to be a nun, admiring their purity and rigid self-discipline and, perhaps, influenced by her mother's courage in the face of her fatal illness. As she prepared for her confirmation, she claimed she developed a crush on Jesus Christ. 'He was like a movie star, my favourite idol of all' and chose Veronica as her confirmation name, as her mother had done, from the legend that St Veronica wiped the sweat from the face of Jesus with her handkerchief during His Journey to Calvary. But on the other hand she loved to have a good time and cause a stir. During one summer vacation at Bay City staying with her grandmother, she had created a big impact by dressing up as a 'ten-cent floozie' (her grandmother's phrase), and feeling, for the first time in her life, that she was really grown up. A childhood friend, Carol Belanger, remembers Madonna's outspokenness in those days: 'Sometimes I'd literally have to put my hand over her mouth to shut her up. She once yelled up and told this group of bikers who were dropping firecrackers on us to knock it off. The next thing I knew one of the biker girls came down and started hitting her in the mouth. We finally got away but Madonna had a black eye and a bruised mouth.'

She had never abandoned the wide range of dancing lessons that she had taken as a child and by the time she was into her early teens was clearly a talented and dedicated dancer, practising for several hours a day when the chance arose. One summer she took part in a local talent competition, choreographing to a record by The Who, dressed in a bikini and fluorescent body paint.

Tony was determined that all his children should work hard at their lessons: he took a great interest in their schooling and rewarded them financially if they did well, and punished them with extra chores if they did badly. Madonna attended three Catholic junior schools in Rochester and Bay City – St Andrews, St Fredericks and the Sacred Heart Academy – before moving on to Rochester Adams High at the age of twelve. She was a good pupil, always getting decent grades, but it was dancing in which she excelled. Her ability ensured she was always picked for school productions, notably playing Eliza Doolittle in *My Fair Lady*. During her eighth grade, Madonna's penchant for the unusual was demonstrated by her appearance in her first film: an amateur short Super-8 directed by a school friend, in which an egg was fried on her stomach. This was probably a visual interpretation of Paul Simon's then current single 'Mother and Child Reunion' (a bizarre concept of an egg-and-chicken meal, the chicken being the mother of the egg, both of which were about to be consumed).

From her father, Madonna inherited a prodigious capacity for hard work. As the sixth child of an immigrant family, he had pulled himself up to earn a degree and a good job by consistent application to the task in hand and to him sloth was perhaps the most deadly of the deadly sins. Having decided from an early age that she was going to be a dancer, Madonna worked hard at keeping fit throughout her teens and her obsession with fitness is still with her to this day. Perhaps another reason for this obsession can be found in the trauma of her mother's early death. Maybe, she thought, I can avoid a similar fate if I take care of my body. She tried drugs, along with the other kids, but hated them so much that she abandoned them immediately; similarly, alcohol.

At the age of fourteen, Madonna started to go out with boys and was very popular with them from the outset. Having three brothers, she understood boys and was not at all shy or awkward in their company. She also knew very well how to flirt with men, after all her early practice with her father. Some mistook her openness for promiscuity but, in fact, nothing could have been further from the truth. And when, having had such good fun all evening, the boys went away without getting what they thought was being handed to them on a plate, some of them turned on her and spread rumours that she was 'easy'. As it happened, the first boy Madonna went to bed with had been her boyfriend for a long time and she felt she was in love with him. His name was Russell and he was two years her senior.

There may also have been another reason for her dedication to dancing: at home, she was still obliged to do chores, look after her young stepbrother and sister and adhere to a 9.30 p.m. curfew. Away from home, she could be free from such duties and her dancing provided her with a legitimate reason to leave; after all, she had long harboured a dream of a showbusiness career.

In tenth grade, Madonna got to know a girl who was a serious student of ballet. Madonna has recalled that she was attracted to her because she looked smarter than the average girl but in an interesting, offbeat manner. Naturally, she was intrigued by this girl, and she persuaded her to take her along and introduce her to the ballet class she attended at Rochester, which was run by Christopher Flynn. At this time, Flynn was in his forties, a confident and self-assured homosexual. His school specialized in modern dance rather than classical ballet and he was very demanding of his pupils, charismatic and greatly admired by them. He was certainly the first fully mature artistic person that Madonna had met and he came to play the most influential part in her life at that time. She decided then and there that she wanted to study with him and has subsequently claimed that he was her 'saviour'.

Urbane, artistic, experienced and professional, Flynn was Madonna's 'introduction to glamour and sophistication' as she put it, and he took her 'to all the gay discotheques in downtown Detroit. Men were doing poppers and going crazy. They were all dressed really well and were more free in themselves than all the blockhead football players I met in High School.' But her relationship with Christopher Flynn was a two-way affair: he has described her as 'one of the best students I've had, a very worldly sort of woman even as a child. We would go to gay bars and she and I would go out and dance our asses off. People would clear away and let her go.' He was her Svengali, her route to another world; he found her fresh and exciting and uniquely talented.

All Madonna's hard work at High School paid off: her graduation marks, combined with her talent for dancing, ensured that she was awarded a full scholarship to the Performing Arts School of the

University of Michigan at Ann Arbor. It was a four-year scholarship. She took dance, music theory and art history, together with a Shakespearean course, as well as continuing to attend Christopher Flynn's ballet class in whatever remained of her free time. University expanded Madonna's experience enormously. At the hub of an artistic environment, her dress and behaviour verged on the bohemian. Some nights she would go to the 'Blue Frogge' nightclub on the edge of the campus, where she met a part-time waiter, a tall and good-looking black youth called Steve Bray. Steve was a talented musician, a fine drummer, but at first their relationship was more physical than musical.

Her life now was a very different one from that she had experienced at home in Rochester. She was also able to travel a bit, going to a dance workshop course at Duke University in Durham, North Carolina, a journey of about 600 miles and the furthest away from home she had ever been. This course lasted six weeks and turned out to have far-reaching consequences for her. While doing the workshop, she learned that six students were to be selected and awarded a place at Alvin Ailey's Dance Studio in New York, which was run by Ailey and Pearl Lang. Pearl Lang, now fifty-five years old, had studied dance under the legendary Martha Graham and been principal dancer in her Company from 1942 to 1952. Martha Graham, the leader of the Modern Dance Movement (as it came to be called) in America was a remarkable woman, who finally retired from dancing at the age of seventy-seven. Her ballets were almost invariably danced barefoot and her choreography demanded considerable physical strength. Graham's importance in twentieth-century American dance cannot be over-emphasized and for Madonna, the chance to study with Graham's leading dancer was one that she was determined not to miss. She took it by the direct expedient of saying to one of the judges that having seen a Pearl Lang performance, 'She's the only one I want to work with.' Even Madonna's brimful self-confidence took a momentary downward fall when the lady replied, 'I am Pearl Lang.'

Pearl Lang was intrigued by Madonna's determination, to say nothing of her ability, and recalled later that, 'Madonna simply has the magical quality that a great artist needs.' Quite clearly, therefore, at this stage of her life (Madonna was still only eighteen) the young girl's talent was there for those with eyes to see. It is not difficult to imagine the state of tingling excitement in which Madonna returned to Michigan and informed everyone that she had decided to leave university and to go and study in New York.

Her decision was greeted with wide disapproval, from the University authorities and especially from her father Tony, who was most anxious that his daughter should at least complete the course and then perhaps try New York. But Madonna was encouraged by Christopher Flynn, who told her that she should do what she really thought was best for her. With such support from the man who had probably done more than anyone else to develop her artistic leanings in the previous year, Madonna saved enough money to buy a one-way ticket and leave her with about $45 spending money, and took the plane for her first-ever flight, of 502 miles, to New York. Having arrived in the Big Apple Madonna caught a cab from the airport for the ride to 'the middle of everything' as she put it, from where she wanted to start. The cab driver put her down in Times Square. Now, cut off from family, friends and everyone else she had previously known, and with just thirty-five dollars in her purse, Madonna had arrived to seek her fame and fortune in New York City. From now on, she was on her own.

2
THE LOWER EAST SIDE

Nearly all great cities have a definable 'heart', the part – usually somewhere near the centre – where the visitor can stand and truly feel that they are at the very kernel of the city. In London, perhaps it is Piccadilly Circus; in Paris, maybe the area surrounding Nôtre Dame. Most cities, also, have more than one famous landmark which could vie for such a description, but few New Yorkers would doubt that the heart of New York City, for the first-time visitor, is Times Square.

The junction of Broadway, Seventh Avenue and 42nd Street is truly a vibrant and amazing place, dazzling in its constant activity and brilliantly myriad lights. The pace of the city that truly never sleeps, the very electricity which seems to rise up from the paving-stones on the sidewalks, the extraordinary ethnic mix of race, religion and society – New York's stunning life never fails to exert the most profound impact on the imaginations of those who visit it for the first time. It is customary to fall in love with New York, especially Manhattan, but it is not the only brightly lit big city that has attracted hopeful young people like moths to a flame, and has consumed those who cannot survive the pace as surely as if in some blazing inferno.

The effect on the eighteen-year-old Madonna was immediate and overwhelming. After getting out of the cab, she stood on the sidewalk for some time, drinking in the sights and sounds of this amazing hub of activity. Although it was a summer afternoon, and the lights were awaiting nightfall to make their proper impact, Madonna stood open-mouthed at the height of the buildings and all that was going on around her. Even here, she stood apart from the crowd. She had wisely taken an overcoat for protection from the penetrating New York winters but had no space in her suitcase to pack it, so she was wearing it. A young girl of five feet four-and-a-half inches, wearing a heavy winter coat in the middle of Times Square on a summer afternoon will still attract the occasional glance: as she moved up Broadway, she noticed a man following her.

'Hi,' she said.

'Hi,' he replied, and continued, 'Why are you walking around with a winter coat and a suitcase? Why don't you go home and get rid of it?'

Madonna saw no reason to lie: 'I don't live anywhere.'

The stranger replied: 'Well, you can stay at my apartment.'

And she did. In fact, Madonna stayed with the man for two weeks; as she said, 'He didn't try to rape me or anything. He showed me where everything was and he fed me breakfast. It was perfect.'

After two weeks, Madonna found herself a room, at 242 East Fourth Street, near the East Village, the Bowery and New York University. It was a dump, as she recalled later: 'I knew it was the absolute worst neighbourhood I could live in.'

'When I first arrived I was really lonely. I didn't have any money and I didn't have anywhere to stay. You're really confined, you're a small fish in a big sea instead of a big fish in a little pond. I was getting lost on the subway trains all the time. You really have to gear yourself to your work, that's your focal point and that's your security. Slowly I got to know it and became secure and now it's odd to think how scared I was.'

Even the most self-assured young person would have felt scared in such circumstances. But Madonna was distinguished from the thousands of young people who hit New York without money every year and are dragged into a downward spiral of drugs and prostitution, because she had a reason for being there. She was one of only six students chosen for a work-study scholarship with Pearl Lang and Alvin Ailey, and she was later asked to take classes with the Theatre's third company, still under Pearl Lang's tutelage. Pearl Lang said later: 'She was an exceptional dancer. Many dancers can kick and exhibit acrobatic body control, but that is just run-of-the-mill, taken for granted. Madonna had the power, the intensity to go beyond mere physical performances into

19

something far more exciting. That intensity is the first thing I look for in a dancer, and Madonna had it.'

But one cannot eat talent, and Madonna survived by taking menial jobs in fast-food outlets (which had the added bonus of free food). 'I was fired from a long succession of ratty jobs,' is how she succinctly puts it. Once, whilst serving at Dunkin' Donuts, she lost her job for squirting a stream of jam over a customer who was getting rude. Other jobs similarly tried her patience and none of them lasted long. And so, eventually, she undertook something which, in later years, came to haunt her: nude modelling.

In the event, she did both art modelling for drawing classes, and photographic modelling. As she later recalled, 'For years, when I first moved to New York, I modelled for a lot of art schools, for the drawing and painting classes: the nude is an essential part of study for a person beginning to study art; they have to draw the anatomy of the human body. Because I was a dancer I was in really good shape, and I was slightly underweight so you could see my muscle definition and my skeleton. I was one of their favourite models because I was so easy to draw.

'I got paid very well for that, versus having to work eight hours in a restaurant. I could work in a school for three hours, then take dance classes all day, then do my show at night if I was performing. I'd be making money and not working that many hours. So, when I did this a lot of people wanted me to start modelling privately for them. They had little get-togethers on the weekends, say three people in the class . . . the smaller the class the better. I could hang out a lot more and work a lot less. So I got to know these people in a friendly kind of way. They became like surrogate mothers and fathers for me, they took care of me. Then, what would happen is, they'd say they knew a great photographer and he's doing an exhibit on nudes and he'd like to do some pictures. So I'd get involved with photographers that way. Then he would turn me on to somebody else, and for the photography sessions I'd be paid a lot more than for drawing. I consider the nude a work of art. I don't see pornography in Michelangelo, and I likened what I was doing to that.'

Such peripheral activities could never obscure the fact that dancing was her life, her main interest. As a dance student she was naturally interested in music as well and her tastes by this time spanned classical as well as pop and jazz. In fact, Madonna has acquired a surprisingly detailed knowledge of some classical composers, particularly Bach, Vivaldi, Handel, Mozart, Chopin and Brahms, who are her favourites. Curiously, each of these composers exhibits a strong formal sense, and a clarity and directness of expression, which in some ways can be seen to have similarities with Madonna's later work in the musical field. Those composers who are emotionally more subjective in their music – Tchaikovsky, Mahler, and even in popular terms (though not in strict musical ones) Beethoven, did not appeal so strongly to her.

In spite of whatever cultural irrigation nurtured Madonna in her early months in New York there remained little that was admirable about her living environment near the Bowery. Regarded as the Skid Row of New York, in the late 1970s the area around Fourth Street was still that to which the failures and drop-outs of the city gravitated; it needed toughness to live there. As Madonna confessed, she had to adopt a tough shell as a defence: 'I used to be just a brazen, crazy lass, and I went out of my way to get attention from people. I would wear one orange sock and one purple one. I went out of my way to make statements with my clothing and obviously I got looks from people . . . I brazenly looked people in the eye when I walked down the streets in New York. I loved getting dressed up and going out on the street and walking around. I didn't have money to take cabs then, so I took subway trains a lot and I loved seeing the visual effect I had on people.' This was the time of the punk movement in Britain and in the States and although Madonna was not actively 'punk' in her musical tastes and her attitudes, her dress certainly showed some influences from them – the torn clothes, trash hair and safety pins for jewellery.

Whatever effect Madonna may have had on her fellow citizens, to Tony Ciccone she was still at heart his 'Little Nonni', and one can imagine the effect her living accommodation had on him when he was able to visit her from time to time. Madonna recalls: 'When my father came to visit, he was mortified. The place was crawling with cockroaches, there were winos in the hallways, and the entire place smelled like stale beer.' Tony's mortification was perhaps the more intense when one considers that for him, Madonna's dancing had always been in the nature of a hobby. He still thought that she ought to have obtained a good all-round education, to have got a good job and to have secured her future. As far as he was concerned, dancing was not that, and in so far as it affected her day-to-day life, he remained unconvinced that it showed any signs of providing her with security.

As the weeks passed into months, and the new year of 1977 dawned, the hard facts of her chosen profession began to assume greater practical reality for her. At any one time, there are many more dancers seeking work than there are dancing jobs. A full-time dancing career was extremely rare, and, because of the very nature of the work, was always fraught with the physical danger of injury and an immediate cessation of that work. Madonna was told that, on average, a dancer would have to wait about five years before any kind of notable chance arose. Perhaps, at first, she felt such strictures did not apply to her but eventually the months of poor accommodation, irregular eating, and faintly dubious extra-curricular activities, to say nothing of her father's admonishments, led her to realize that, whilst using her dancing ability and sense of rhythm, and her genuine love of music, she might be able to find another outlet within the entertainment profession in which to make her mark.

Her frustration at the lack of opportunity for professional dancers led her to see her fellow-students in a new light: 'It really annoyed me that most of the dancers I knew had such a simple-minded view of life. They were really closed up. They got up early, took dance classes all day, and then they went to rehearsal and ate healthy food. Then they went home and went to bed early. They did this every day and they didn't know anything about music or art . . . Most of the kids that I knew who were in my ballet class . . . were little bratty girls who stared at themselves in the mirror all day.

'I found myself doing the same thing, ultimately, that I did when I was living in Detroit. I started rebelling and wanting to get out. All these girls would come to class with black leotards and pink tights and their hair put up in buns with little flowers in it. So I cut my hair really short and I'd grease it so it would be sticking up, and I'd rip my tights so there were runs all over them and I'd make a big cut down the middle of my leotard and put safety pins all the way up it. Anything to stand out from them and say, "I'm not like you, OK. I'm taking dance classes and everything but I'm not stuck here like you." Eventually I said to myself, "Well, if you don't like it, Madonna, do what you want to do, you know you can dance. You've made a lot of friends, you know musicians, so go do what you want to do."

'That's when I started exploring other territories and quit going to dance classes every day.'

An out-going live-wire such as Madonna was never short of boyfriends, and she was just as much an attractive personality and precocious individual on the East Side as she had been elsewhere. In addition, her chosen profession was cross-cultural, for dance embraces movement, design, all kinds of music and fashion, often a literary story and theatrical spectacle, tradition (in classical ballet) as well as innovation (in extemporization). Consequently, her friends and associates were drawn almost exclusively from students of other arts (more than once, she has described her social milieu at the time as, 'Like something from a production of *Fame*'). One close platonic friend was Martin Burgoyne, an illustrator who worked as a bartender at the nightclub Studio 54. Madonna was working at the time as a hat-check girl at the Russian Tea Room but they met while partying after work and got on immediately.

At around this time, spray-can art and break-dancing were becoming fashionable and Madonna numbered amongst her friends several who were inveterate graffiti artists. She would sometimes hang out at the famous The Roxy disco, then one of New York City's hottest spots, situated at 515 West 18th Street, halfway between Tenth and Eleventh Avenues. In those days, The Roxy would be packed each night with breakers and graffiti artists, and each regular used to have their own phrase which they would graphically spray on the walls of the main dance floor. Madonna's was 'Boy Toy', which she rather liked, and later on she had this phrase, with her design, made into a belt buckle.

Perhaps her growing impatience with what must have seemed an interminable length of time to wait for recognition led her to get into, 'The habit of carrying markers and writing my name everywhere' – an outward and visible sign of her frustration, made more so by her Leonine personality, the need to have her talents recognized. It was at this time that she met Norris Burroughs, the leading graffiti T-shirt designer. They were instantly attracted to each other and interested in each other, and although their relationship only lasted for three months they did live together for most of that time. It all ended amicably when Burroughs threw a party to which he had invited the Gilroy brothers, Dan and Ed. Norris was trying to ease Madonna out of his life, and his home, without any hard feelings and he thought that Dan would be ideal to take over as her next boyfriend. He prepared the ground for them both by extolling the other's virtues to each in turn for several days before the party. When they were introduced, Madonna's first words to him were, 'Aren't you going to kiss me?' Fair enough, but Gilroy recalled that, 'At the party, she was wearing these clothes that looked like a clown outfit. She didn't make a huge impression on me at first because she seemed sort of draggy, like depressed or something.'

But within a few days, Madonna had dated Dan a couple of times and had become enthralled by his varied artistic skills. He had a music-rehearsal studio in what was once a synagogue in the Corona district of the borough of Queens, just across the East River, and not too far from Shea Stadium. Shortly after they met, Madonna went to live there and began exploring the instruments in the studio.

She had not abandoned dancing entirely, but had reduced her classes to a minimum, prior to feeling her way into something new. In her search for a different performing outlet, she had answered an ad seeking backing dancers for a major tour being undertaken by the then highly successful Patrick Hernandez (known as 'Patch'). Hernandez was a German singer who had had a massive transcontinental hit with 'Born To Be Alive' and his French management were in New York looking to put together a Las Vegas revue-style show which would feature Hernandez, who, despite whatever vocal gifts he had, was not a dancer.

Hernandez's French managers, Jean-Claude Pellerin and Jean van Lieu, were immediately impressed by Madonna's performance at her audition and asked her to come back the following day. The Frenchmen were completely taken by her, and after a few moments' discussion between themselves decided that she had star potential. Far from backing Patch, Madonna, they felt, could be groomed into 'the next Edith Piaf' and when she returned, they offered her what must have seemed to her like the moon.

Madonna recalls, 'Finally, they took me into this room and said, "We don't want you to do the revue, we want to make you a star." They were based in Paris and they wanted me to go there and study with a vocal coach while they found material for me. I'd never been abroad before and I wanted to see a bit of

24

the world. I was in seventh heaven. I kept thinking "Somebody noticed me."'

She would be given an apartment, a good one, with a maid, a singing teacher, and generous expenses. It was, quite literally, an astounding offer, a remarkable stroke of good fortune, which she could not, under any circumstances, refuse. Nor did she, but it meant her new-found relationship with Dan, and the very much less material opportunities which might come her way by being with him, had to come to an end. Their last few weeks together were pleasantly idyllic: they both recall them with affection, days of doing as much together as they could, just being in each other's company, eating, playing or listening to music, or going to movies or out in the nearby Corona Park, and coming home together at nights. Would they ever meet again, and if so, when, and in what circumstances?

Madonna finally gave up her dancing lessons early in 1979 and, eagerly looking forward to this extraordinary opportunity which had befallen her and with a sad backward glance at Dan Gilroy, she boarded the plane which would take her to a new country and a new life.

3
THE BREAKFAST CLUB

Paris was another world. Here, physically removed from the East Side, Brooklyn, boys, dance lessons, fast-food outlets, discos and the teeming life which had so struck her on her arrival in Times Square, Madonna was in Europe for the first time, in the heart of one of its most beautiful cities, and being treated like royalty. She recalls that at first, 'living in Paris was like a French movie'. Her benefactors obviously thought they had discovered a major star and set about grooming her for stardom in their own manner. The problem, which soon began to make itself manifest, was that their perception of how a star should be so prepared differed profoundly from Madonna's.

She could not complain about her lifestyle. Ensconced in an elegant Montmartre apartment, with a daily maid, a chauffeur, tutors, and generous personal expenses, Jean Claude Pellerin and Jean van Lieu ensured that she had the best they could provide. But since she didn't speak French, she soon began to feel a bit cut off; her benefactors spoke English but the maid and the chauffeur did not and the demanding voice and dancing coaches engaged to train her came to the apartment to work, not to chat.

Madonna did work, however: the Hernandez tour embraced North Africa, and she went along to Tunisia as a member of the backing dance group. Writers were engaged specially for her: 'She's a Real Disco Queen' was the result, but it was a manufactured piece of aural wallpaper, none-too-well designed to judge from her comments: 'I overdubbed vocals on to some already-recorded disco tracks, but basically it was pretty boring.'

She was taken to fashionable couturiers, and to stylish restaurants, but as the weeks and months went by, with few tangible results that Madonna could see, she began to feel uneasy at the situation. A stranger in a strange land, whenever she ventured to complain that things did not seem to be happening for her – at least, in the way in which she imagined they ought to be happening – the two managers would give her more money. She began to rebel against her situation, in small ways at first – for example ordering three desserts as the whole meal in a top-class restaurant, thereby embarrassing her hosts and the restaurateur.

Occasionally, when she could slip away from what she increasingly felt was little more than an open prison, she would gravitate to the less well-off, more street-wise members of Parisian society. This was not difficult to do in Montmartre, especially in the area around the Gare-du-Nord, and she took up with a group of Algerian and Vietnamese youths who lived on the edge of the law and terrorized local residents as they roared round the centre of Paris on their motorbikes, out-manoeuvring the occasional police vehicles. In their company, Madonna felt more at home than in the strange and false situation she had been thrust into of the young lady with everything. She remembered what her father had taught her: 'If it's handed to you on a plate, it's not going to last.'

As time went by, Madonna's feelings of frustration were made more acute by a growing sense of homesickness. This was heightened by the cards and letters she would get, sometimes cryptic and in little more than telegram style, from Dan Gilroy. 'He was my saving grace, his letters were so funny,' she remembered later. 'He would paint a picture of an American flag, and write over it, like it was from the President "We miss you. You must return to America."'

The core of her frustration was simple: as she said, 'I wanted to work; I got miserable in Paris without doing anything.' Furthermore, almost as a last straw, illness intervened. She contracted what at first appeared to be a very heavy cold, but in fact it was a form of viral pneumonia – not serious, but of some concern. When she had recovered sufficiently, she begged the two French managers to let her go back to America for a week's holiday. Whether she was actually planning to escape at that stage is not clear but as soon as they bought her a ticket and she landed back on American soil, Madonna decided that she was not returning to Paris. There was nothing to hold her there as the Frenchmen had not made her sign a contract, and for all their wealth and good connections in the European music business, things were just not happening fast enough for her.

Once back in New York, she made three calls: the first, to Dan Gilroy, asking if they could take up where they had left off a mere five months earlier (although it seemed like years to her), and the second to the managers in Paris, telling them that she was not returning. Perhaps they were relieved; they had invested a fair amount of money in Madonna, but their realism must have told them that she was becoming increasingly unco-operative and was not interested in moving in the direction they wanted her to go. The third call was to Martin Burgoyne. Dan had been a little uncertain about letting Madonna just come round and move in as though nothing had happened; he was pleased she was back in New York, but could not offer her accommodation immediately. Martin, by all accounts a quiet, pleasant individual in his late teens, could and she moved in immediately, secure at least in the knowledge that there would be no underlying sexual relationship. After several weeks of staying at Martin's place, Madonna went to live with Dan. Martin had proved to be a good and practical friend, which is just what she needed at the time to get herself together after the French débâcle.

It would be quite wrong, however, to claim that the five months Madonna spent in Paris were entirely wasted. She could hardly have failed to profit from the experience, and the voice coaching she had been given proved highly beneficial. She knew that she could dance – it was that talent which had got her to France in the first place and now she knew that she also had a distinctive voice which had benefited from professional training. She had had additional performing experience in public in pop/rock venues (admittedly not in major cities, but the grounding was valuable). Now back in her own environment, she was raring to go.

Dan Gilroy claims that she had 'caught the music bug in Paris'. Her next goal had taken shape: she knew she wanted to be a singer. She has said that she, 'Grew up wanting to perform. I have to concentrate on one thing at a time; that got me to the audition which got me to Paris and on my return I concentrated for a year or more practising writing, singing and playing. I really lived off the good graces of other people.'

She was given the free run of Dan's studio and started off by teaching herself to play the drums. Dan had a theory that anyone who had a sense of timing could be a drummer and Madonna's dancing experience had certainly given her that attribute. She also had very highly developed muscular co-ordination and the ability to apply herself to the task in hand and practise till she dropped, so within a short time she had become a proficient drummer. Next she got Dan to show her some simple chords and progressions on the guitar, and devoted her time to practising at that instrument and teaching herself to play.

It was not long before she decided that she wanted to form a group. Dan's brother Ed was a rhythm guitarist and lead singer; Dan was the lead guitarist, and Madonna would play drums. A dancer friend of hers, Angie Smit, joined the fledgling band as bass guitarist. With the members of the group more or less in place, it was down to rehearsal. Once again, Madonna's driving ambition came into its own. Dan said, 'Rehearse, rehearse, rehearse; she's a real workaholic.' They would begin rehearsing during the evening and play right through the night until exhaustion took over and they made their way to the neighbouring International Pancake House for breakfast. From this ritual came the name of the band: The Breakfast Club.

Next Madonna turned to keyboard playing, perhaps regretting that she had not continued her piano lessons as a child. But, after several weeks of more constant daily practice alone and with the band at nights, she soon mastered the keyboards and began to try her hand at writing songs.

She has said of this period that, 'It was one of the happiest times of my life. I really felt loved. Sometimes I'd write some sad songs and he [Dan Gilroy] would sit there and cry. Very sweet.' Gilroy himself has described those weeks as 'Good times that came from a mishmash of fun, music, friendship and romance.'

Within a few months, The Breakfast Club was ready to perform and they managed to get bookings at 'all the Lower East Side hellholes', as Madonna described them. These included such places as Max's Kansas City and C.B.G.B. – though they were not the worst.

Having got the band together and got it performing, the next thing was to get it noticed, and as Dan Gilroy says, 'She'd be up in the morning, she'd have a quick cup of coffee and then sit by the phone and call up everybody – everyone from local record dealers to potential management.' Perhaps now the band was beginning to mean more to Madonna than it did to the others (for both Dan and Ed Gilroy had daytime jobs) and she has freely admitted that she, 'Took advantage of the situation. I wanted to know everything they knew because I knew I could make it work to my benefit. I was just a lot more goal-orientated and commercial than they were.'

It quickly became obvious that one member of the band was really not putting in as much work as the others. Angie Smit, according to Dan Gilroy, would hardly play any music live. 'After all our rehearsals, her performance consisted mainly of standing there staring at the audience. Occasionally,' with a heavy emphasis on 'occasionally', 'she might play a note or two.' Angie got a lot of attention on stage, however, because she wore clothes of such a revealing nature that, as Gilroy continued, 'People looked at us like a strip show.' This attention was detracting from whatever musical merits the band had, and Madonna began to get increasingly impatient with their lack of a competent bass player. Perhaps she also resented the other female member of the band attracting all the attention. At any rate, it was soon made clear that if Angie could not or would not change she would have to leave, and after a few weeks she did.

Next, Madonna decided that she needed to take another step towards her ultimate ambition of being a singer and she managed to persuade Dan ('Having begged for ages,' as he recalled) to write several songs for her to perform with the band. She explains 'I was always thinking, I want to be a singer in this group too. And they didn't need another singer.' At first, her appearance with the band caused a considerable stir, for after playing drums for most of the set, Madonna would leave the kit and come to the front to do her songs. Such an unusual and attention-getting procedure was distinctive at first, but after a while it was difficult to know who the punters had come to see, for Madonna's performances were markedly different as a singer from those the band gave when she was the drummer.

Dan began to feel himself torn between two very important people in his life: Madonna, his protégée in many ways and his live-in girlfriend, and his brother Ed. The nights of singing had convinced her that she was no longer interested in being a drummer: that part of her career had been valuable experience and very useful to her, but she had to have the upper hand, she had to be the lead singer, the star of the group. The egalitarian basis on which The Breakfast Club had been formed had changed as Madonna's priorities overtook those of her partners; by the end of 1979 and the beginning of 1980, the split had become permanent as Madonna realized that rather than revolutionize The Breakfast Club, she was going to have to leave and form her own band.

Madonna had come to New York in the summer of 1976, and less than three years later she was in Paris, being groomed for stardom. After five months of that, she had turned her back on what was potentially a golden opportunity and during virtually the whole of 1979 had worked extremely hard to gain proficiency as a drummer, guitarist, keyboard player and rock singer. Perhaps, with these myriad experiences allied to her driving ambition, there was comparatively little risk: she had everything she needed now, had it within her, to move forward to the one thing she wanted most of all – recognition of her talents.

Dan was at first disconsolate when she left: 'I missed her very much. It had been a good year. Having Madonna there had been a bonus. There was the normal separation anxiety, of course, but I think we both knew our relationship didn't have a feeling of permanency in it.'

The Breakfast Club continued, but Madonna was once again entirely on her own. She returned to live in the infested apartment blocks and the itinerant jobs she had known two-and-a-half years earlier but this time she had a real goal. She wasted no time in gathering around her a miscellaneous crew of professional and semi-professional musicians, with herself as lead singer and guitarist. She also found a garage in Queens in which they could rehearse, but there were still problems. Her new drummer, Mike Monahan, was engaged to be married within a few months and was very likely to leave, and Madonna found it difficult to inspire the necessary feeling of unity and the same dreams and ambitions in each member of the band. The result was that the personnel changed regularly, and so did the name of the band. At first they were called The Millionaires, and then Modern Dance (an acknowledgement of Pearl Lang's mentor, Martha Graham) and finally Emmy, the pet-name by which Dan Gilroy had called Madonna and a contraction of the third name the band had, Emmenon. What she really needed was another strong personality with whom she could work to join the band and stick with it, to provide some musical continuity. By an extraordinary quirk of fate, when Mike Monahan duly left after his marriage, she received a call from her old friend, Steve Bray, the waiter-drummer she had met at the Blue Frogge nightclub at the University of Michigan. He wanted to come to New York and could she help? She certainly could. As Bray recalls, 'I found that, oddly enough, she needed a drummer at that very moment, so I said, "Fine, I'll be there next week."'

Although other members of Emmy continued to come and go from time to time, as is the norm in the peripatetic life of those on the lower rungs of the music business ladder, together they had a base on which to start building up a repertoire. Their bass guitarist, Gary Burtle, was also a constant member, but there was no question that Madonna was now the leading light. Steve created a small home studio in which Madonna worked – sometimes on her own, sometimes with him – at writing songs, while they continued to play an irregular succession of twenty-five-dollar-a-night gigs at seedy venues.

Every day, Madonna would scour the trade newspapers for snippets of information and one day a small ad seeking hopefuls to appear in a new avant-garde film caught her eye. On impulse, she decided to apply but spent some days drafting her letter, which was handwritten, not typed, and which whilst basically accurate glossed over certain aspects of her earlier life. She sent it to the writer and director of the film, Stephen John Lewicki, who was then in his final year at the University of New York's Film School and who later obtained a philosophy degree from Columbia University. He was attracted by her unconventional approach – written in a matter-of-fact, slightly chatty manner, quite different from the usual typed data, and the photograph she enclosed, of her sitting on a bus applying lipstick with one finger. He says, 'Her approach was strange, very strange, but I decided to follow up on it.' Her unconventionality matched his own, for his auditions tended to take the form of a conversation on neutral ground. Lewicki chose Washington Square, then – around the arch – a burgeoning venue for street break-dancers. 'From the moment I met her, I knew she was a star.' Lewicki had received over one hundred applications for the part, but, 'She fitted the role perfectly, and had a riveting personality,' he recalled. 'She has the charisma that makes a star a star.'

The film, naturally a low-budget short (it runs for sixty minutes), brought her little money – one hundred dollars was her first and final payment – but priceless experience. In it, Madonna played the role of Bruna, 'In post-punk New York . . . who's a dominatrix.' Bruna lives with an equally uncertain character, Dashiel, and they both hustle for money and food. But Bruna gets more than she bargained for when she is raped by an older man. She and Dashiel vow revenge on him and they eventually track the man down and Dashiel kills him, the couple revelling in their ritual. The very title, *A Certain Sacrifice* recalls the 1958 Jean Negulesco film *A Certain Smile* based on the novel by Françoise Sagan in which a young girl, a coquettish personality, falls in love with her womanizing uncle. The film version of this book sanitizes the original story and the theme of *A Certain Sacrifice* can at one level be seen to carry the original Sagan story several stages further in a kind of bizarre, deformed, mirror-image. No one would claim that *A Certain Sacrifice* is a profound work of art, but without any special pleading it demonstrates that Madonna could certainly act: her performance does not betray inexperience. The film was a first-shot for many of the people involved and it does have a few rough edges, but although some have described it as a 'soft-porn movie', it is no such thing. Obviously, with such a story-line (Bruna dominates men as her sex slaves as well as getting raped) sex is not too far away, but Lewicki shows remarkable restraint in the visual portrayal of the steamier scenes.

As so often in her life, Madonna had been immediately given an opportunity which others might have taken years to achieve. Lewicki spoke of her at this time: 'Madonna is a very complex individual. As an actress she is the consummate professional: on time, understands her role, always delivers her lines. But she has an incredible swing of moods in her personal life. She can express deep love then fiery hatred for the same thing – or person – within a few minutes.'

In fact, Lewicki seems to have had a closer personal relationship with Madonna than most directors do with their leading ladies. He admits that they had 'a really flirtatious relationship' and on one occasion, on set, a witness reported seeing him licking blueberry yoghurt out of her ear. The film was finished by the middle of 1980 but it did not receive any kind of general release and it only came out on video in 1985.

33

Meanwhile, Madonna and Steve Bray were still working hard, writing songs and trying to keep their band together. They managed to rent facilities in the Music Building, a large twelve-storey building which served as a kind of unofficial University of Rock Music in New York City. The place was peopled by hundreds of aspiring rock musicians, all anxious to get that big break, and who were rehearsing, meeting, recording, talking about rock music twenty-four hours a day. Occasionally, Madonna and Steve would pick up some extra musicians there to do an Emmy gig, and they both spent a great deal of time at the Building. One day, Madonna saw a young man getting out of the elevator. Acting on impulse, she said to him, 'Hey, you look like John Lennon.'

It was not Lennon, who would shortly meet his death at the hand of an assassin outside his New York apartment, but a man named Adam Alter. He was in the Building on the look-out for likely talent to sign to his Gotham Productions Music Company, which embraced rehearsal studios and a management company and which he had, in fact, formed only a few weeks before. Yet again, Madonna had struck lucky at just the right time: as Alter himself recalled, 'It was good timing.' He was sufficiently impressed with Madonna's enthusiasm and personality to take one of the demo tapes she had made with Steve Bray to his partner, Camille Barbone, who was similarly taken with Madonna and her songs. Alter continued, 'Right from the first, Camille and I were certain that Madonna was destined for great things. We wanted her to become a rock and pop multimedia superstar appealing to everyone from little kids to adult theatregoers. To say we believed in her is an understatement: we signed her immediately.'

At last, Madonna was contracted to professional management, and coincidentally discovered that Camille Barbone shared the same birthday as her: Camille was eight years Madonna's senior and during the coming weeks came to be more than a manager. 'I discovered that she didn't have any money and hadn't eaten for three days,' Camille recounted. 'Madonna had a guitar but the neck was broken. She had a bicycle but that had a flat tyre. I felt sorry for her, she was really in need.'

The Gotham Productions Studio was quite well established and had been used by Johnny Winter and David Johansen, as well as by Melba Moore: a clause in Madonna's contract with Gotham gave her the use of this studio, a regular salary of a hundred dollars a week, accommodation in an Upper West Side apartment away from the, 'Place filled with prostitutes, degenerates and escaped convicts' as Adam Alter described her flop-house room. Madonna also had infinitely greater freedom now to choose from the best musicians with which to work, hired by Gotham, but on the stipulation that Steve Bray be retained as her drummer. She also insisted that the band's name be hers – Madonna – and with this demand also met it seemed, at last, that she had just about everything she needed.

Now she could work incessantly, without worrying about money for food or rent – or for rehearsal or studio time. And work she did: whilst Gotham Productions were anxious to get her film or television work, she and Steve Bray spent virtually every waking hour in the studio, writing songs, one after another. The songs themselves, the first products of this contract, were true rocker numbers, and at nights Madonna and Steve (along with the other members of the band) would perform them in a variety of clubs, notably Chase Park, Botany Talk House and My Father's Place. But in early 1981 the raw edges were smoothed as Madonna took to writing ballads rather than hard-driving numbers. Some of her songs at that time sound as though they were influenced by the Police, one of the most successful bands topping the charts at the time.

By this stage, the Emmy-Madonna band was beginning to enjoy something of a following amongst the clientèle of the clubs in which they performed regularly. Madonna was more than able, as she moved into this second-generation post-punk phase, to work with an audience and make them listen to what she wanted them to. This is a crucial point: most striving bands or singers write their own material, but unless they have a record contract and a product on the market it's difficult to hook audiences. That is why many aspiring musicians resort to doing their own versions of current hits, with the result that, no matter how good they are, they inevitably appear as second best. But once an audience-following is built up, and the audiences like the new material that the band is producing, then the artist has a chance of breaking through. Madonna was aware of the power she had over her audiences, no matter how small and cult-orientated they were. In addition, Camille thought Madonna was sensational and lost no time in telling all and sundry of her beliefs, and in bolstering Madonna's ego with dreams of stardom.

So far, so good, but Gotham Productions had as yet seen little return on their investment.

Adam Alter has said that, 'Madonna was a very modest, humble girl when we met her and the two of us treated her like a star before she was a star. Camille especially inflated her head with the star thing in a way that, in retrospect, was unbelievable.' The Gotham money did not come from some bottomless pit, and Madonna could not be supported indefinitely without some income: such returns could most readily be obtained by selling the tapes Madonna and Steve had made for Gotham of four of her songs.

Alter described the situation: 'It all became like a race, the big race to get the big money by selling the tape. We had the star, we had the songs, and everything was right. The only problem was that there were too many egos clashing around. Everyone wanted a piece of Madonna.' The problem became acute: with the best of intentions, Gotham's senior management learned that the road to hell is paved with them. Whilst every effort was made to get them placed with the best possible company, and encouraging noises had been made by senior staff in suitable organizations, Gotham remained unsuccessful. The tapes, by all accounts, were of excellent quality, but the labyrinth of contractual restrictions which now surrounded them made disposing of them difficult. Since Madonna's stardom, it seems probable that they will never be released now.

This contractual stalemate was very frustrating for Madonna and Steve. She also felt that Gotham Productions were trying to push her in the wrong direction musically. Always an inveterate nightclubber with her ear to the ground for the hottest new sounds, Madonna felt that what she wanted to do – and what would be commercially most successful – was her own brand of dance music: 'I've always been into rhythmic music, party music, but Gotham weren't used to that stuff, and although I'd agreed to do rock and roll, my heart was no longer in it. Soul was my main influence and I wanted to approach it from a very simple point of view because I wasn't an incredible musician. I wanted it to be direct. I still loved to dance and all I wanted to do was make a record that I would want to dance to, and people would want to dance to.'

So, after over a year together, Madonna and Gotham split. While she had achieved a following during that time and more valuable experience, financially she was no better off than when she first met Adam Alter. But she did know that Steve and she could put together good tapes and immediately set about putting down four new songs: 'Everybody', 'Burning Up', 'Stay' and 'Ain't No Big Deal'. Madonna now needed someone to do what Gotham had been unable to do and once again, at just the opportune time, a new person entered her life to help her in the right manner. The person was Mark Kamins, who was one of the most fashionable DJs in town, as well as being a record producer. They met at Danceteria, a funky disco spread out over four floors at 30 West 21st Street, in the Chelsea district, where Kamins was resident, and where Madonna was 'tearing up the dance floor' as he put it. She came over and introduced herself, 'then we started going out to clubs together'. As simple as that.

'She had this incredible sense of style,' Kamins has recalled. 'She had an aura.' Within a few days Madonna had played Kamins her tape: he was very impressed and played it at his disco to a tremendous reaction. So impressed was he that he told Michael Rosenblatt, a successful young A-and-R man at Sire Records, about his discovery. Sire was a New Wave label distributed by Warner Brothers, which had made its name by signing some of the major New York acts of the late 1970s, such as the Ramones and Talking Heads.

Rosenblatt has said of his first meeting with Madonna: 'I took Mark up on his offer to introduce me to her. I was out on the town with the guys from Wham! when all of our heads got turned by this incredibly wild-looking, beautiful girl who was on her way up to the DJ booth. I immediately knew it was Madonna, introduced myself, and said, "When you have your tape ready, I'd love to hear it."'

Madonna needed no second bidding: a week later, having done some studio work on the tape, she arrived at Rosenblatt's office with Mark Kamins. From that moment on, things moved with unprecedented speed, for as Michael Rosenblatt recalled: 'I listened to the four cuts on the tape, then I rolled it back and listened to the first song again. That was enough for me.' Within a few moments, Michael had drafted a contract but before Madonna could consider herself signed to Sire Records, the company's president, Seymour Stein, had to give his permission. There was one problem: Stein was at that time in Lenox Hill Hospital recovering from treatment. Michael took the tape to Stein's bedside and played it to him that afternoon. Seymour Stein agreed with Michael's judgment and asked him to bring Madonna and Mark Kamins to the hospital the following day. Stein said he felt he had to shave and comb his hair and get a new dressing-gown, just to meet Madonna.

There probably has never been a more unusual signing in the history of the record business: Madonna has said of the meeting, 'Here I am going into a hospital, to meet this man I've never met before who's sitting there in his jockey shorts with a drip feed in his arm!' And Stein recalls, 'I knew, I just sensed, that there was something that set her apart. She was outgoing, strong, dynamic, and self-assured. I just wanted to rush right in and do a deal.'

The deal he did was for her to make three 12-inch singles of dance-style music for an advance of five thousand dollars. This was by no means a large sum but it was right for the product and for the time, and it gave Madonna what she wanted: a genuine deal with a respected label backed by the resources of one of the largest record and entertainment companies in the world. It was an astonishing development, and a remarkable testimony to her total creative ability.

Seymour Stein reports that Madonna's first words after signing the contract were 'Take me, I'm yours. Now give me the money.'

4
THE FIRST ALBUM

If Madonna had learned anything during the adventures which had befallen her during the previous five years, it was that for things to happen, someone has to make them happen: there's no point sitting around waiting to get lucky. And in the course of making things happen, one or two original plans may have to change.

There is no doubt that Madonna owed Steve Bray a lot. Since she returned from Paris, they had stuck together through thick and thin; he had played with her on just about every gig she had performed, he had written music for her, and it was his input on the demo tapes which had made them sufficiently professional-sounding to have attracted Kamins' attention and Rosenblatt's and Stein's approval. He assumed that he would be producing Madonna's first Sire single, but she had already decided to use Mark Kamins instead. Not that she had anything against Steve but the Sire deal was real business and she needed (as the record company would have rightly demanded) a professional producer. Talented musician though he was, Steve Bray was not yet experienced enough. 'It was really awful,' Madonna says, 'but I just didn't trust him enough.'

Madonna had hoped that Steve would not mind too much since he would be playing on all the tracks but he took the decision badly. They had a massive argument, which led to an immediate and serious split between them, of such proportions that years afterwards neither would talk about the episode. They have now become good friends again but the spring of 1982 is hardly ever mentioned.

In fact Mark Kamins was not very experienced himself. True, he had recently produced an album for Capitol Records but that had not been a major success and he was still essentially a disc-jockey. A record producer needs more than a fashionable pair of ears if he is to bring out in the studio the essential quality of the artist he is responsible for, but at least Kamins knew what was wanted. He got the entire crew together, the musicians, technicians and the instrumentation and took the leading role throughout the first single's production. He was at somewhat of a disadvantage coming in at the end of the line, so to speak; he had not been there when the songs were being written or when they were first recorded, and so could not claim that inner knowledge of the material which both Madonna and Steve Bray naturally possessed.

Equally, Madonna found herself in something of a dilemma. She wasn't convinced that they were using the songs in the best possible way but an artist being given their first big break by a record company is entirely in their hands with regard to the studio work. Even the biggest-selling artists have found themselves a little in awe of the technical side of the recording business when in a studio for real for the first time, and have kept quiet on certain matters when perhaps their instincts told them to speak out. In fact, the Sire Records executives were somewhat disappointed when played the tracks chosen for the first single, 'Ain't No Big Deal' and 'Everybody'. The former had initially been nominated by Michael Rosenblatt as the 'A' side, but it set no-one's pulses racing at the A-and-R/marketing meeting when it was first played. But Rosenblatt recalls that 'The moment I heard "Everybody", I knew that Madonna was off to a great start.'

Having set up sessions for two songs, only one was good enough to be released; but 'Everybody' was so outstanding that Rosenblatt's decision to put it on both sides of the disc was not so bizarre as might at first appear. In truth, he had little choice, but he had every faith in his initial judgment, in the single, and in Madonna's ability to promote it. He has described her attitude to the task in hand: 'Madonna is great. She will do anything to be a star, and that's exactly what I look for in an artist: total co-operation. I want that artist to be there to do whatever I need. Music is a business, after all, and I – my company – spend a fortune, literally, trying to break an act. It is imperative that the artist respects that investment. I try not to deal with artists who think "Music is fun: I can meet people, travel, and get laid a lot." With Madonna, I knew I had someone hot and co-operative, so I planned to build her career with singles, rather than just put an album out right away and run the risk of disaster. Madonna is a unique talent in that she can sing, dance and act, and she looks fabulous. Therefore I was able to do unique planning with her career, and it was incredibly satisfying to see all the pieces fall into place.'

Madonna was more fortunate than she could ever have known to have had someone like Michael Rosenblatt guiding her career from within the record company. People with such understanding and commitment to an artist as he possesses, with the ability not to apply mere formulas to an artist (witness his decision to waste the first song: most A-and-R men would have readily put 'Ain't No Big Deal' on the 'B' side, the repository for most less-than-hit material), to try to mould a recording career around the artist's own qualities, unconcerned with superficial elements of fashion or what is hot that week – such people are rare indeed.

Whether Madonna was fully aware of Rosenblatt's qualities or not at that time, she knew that she had to give the single her total dedication. It was first to be played, appropriately enough, at the Danceteria where Kamins had initially met her. Although the idea was that she should mime to the song, Madonna had other ideas: here was a chance which had to be exploited. She gathered three dancers to back her, one of whom was Martin Burgoyne, and they rehearsed secretly so that when the time came for the Danceteria showcase, with Seymour Stein, Michael Rosenblatt and the Warner Brothers' press and promotion squad in tow out front, the presentation was superb. It formed part of the highly fashionable Haoui Montaug cabaret show 'No Entiendes'. As the Danceteria was regularly packed with taste-makers, and as none of the record men there had ever seen her dance before, they were as thrilled as the audience, who gave her a tremendous ovation.

'Everybody' was not an overnight success but it still sold over 80,000 copies in the US in the first few months after its release, which is certainly a more than respectable figure. It was a big hit in the clubs and most people who had not seen pictures of Madonna assumed that she was a black singer, which accounted in large part for the success the single had in getting played on the rhythm-and-blues stations as well as on dance shows.

Her presentation at the Danceteria and the nationwide airplay the single enjoyed demanded a video. Record companies would not normally make a video for a one-off single without an album to back it up – the cost would not justify it. But Michael Rosenblatt was determined to do all he could for his star and he managed to persuade Ed Steinberg to make a video of 'Everybody' for a modest budget. Such was Steinberg's talent as a video producer that the resultant clip not only fits the music to perfection but gives no hint of a low-budget job. Steinberg has recalled, 'The day I shot "Everybody", one of her three backup dancers didn't show up, which would have cracked most people under the circumstances. Madonna stayed in complete control. Very patiently and very efficiently, she re-choreographed the entire song, following all of my directions for what would and wouldn't work on video. Madonna is hot on video for the simple reason that she is a class act. Working with Madonna is like working with Michael Jackson: she's a uniquely talented performer who can dance, sing and act incredibly well. She's a director's dream because all one needs to do to get a great video is to faithfully record her performance rather than, as with many acts, rely on audiovisual trickery.'

A producer does not need a big budget when you have a supremely talented dancer, who can also choreograph and sing the song she wrote herself. Steinberg's video was instrumental in lifting the sales of the 'Everybody' single to around 250,000; had such sales been concentrated within a shorter period of time and been confined to the national charts, this would have meant a substantial hit. As it was, in national pop chart terms 'Everybody' barely made it, but the total sales meant it made a good return on the initial investment. As Madonna wrote both words and music for 'Everybody', she stood to earn a very respectable sum of money in composer royalties as well.

It was a disappointment for Madonna, and for Michael Rosenblatt, when the head office of Warner Brothers in the UK decided not to release the single there. They felt that 'Everybody' had been produced for a very specific market – the New York club scene – and that while it had managed to break into other areas, the essence of it was dance. They wanted Madonna to go back and produce something that would reach the widest possible audience, that would become a national pop chart hit in the States. Then, they felt, she would be able to make an impression in the UK as well.

Of those who knew her at the time, perhaps Haoui Montaug's

comment that 'She was like a disco act backed by avant-garde dancers – I guess you could say Madonna was the first New Wave disco music' almost defines her newness, her originality. There are some who will maintain that her initial style (as exemplified by 'Everybody' and 'Physical Attraction' – part of the double-A sided second single) was based too closely on Joni Mitchell, Chrissie Hynde, Rickie Lee Jones and Debbie Harry – singers Madonna is known to have admired. 'They were big inspirations to me,' she has said, 'because they were women and they were in charge of what they were doing. They were obviously writing their own lyrics and they had, to me, very strong images and that gave me courage.'

At around this time, Madonna decided that she needed the services of a very experienced and fully professional manager, and her choice fell on Freddy DeMann, who was then manager of Michael Jackson. But she was, in comparison with the superstar, a virtual unknown with little to offer. Nothing daunted, in the summer of 1982 Madonna bought herself a plane ticket to Los Angeles to secure a meeting with DeMann. She succeeded in meeting him and impressed him sufficiently to be able to persuade him to come and see her in action in New York. After seeing her perform, De Mann realized her enormous potential and agreed to look after her affairs: so Madonna was now managed by one of the best people in the business.

Sire and Warner Brothers lost no time in putting the next single in hand, and decided that they needed a new producer to widen Madonna's range. Naturally, Mark Kamins was not thrilled at the news, but he is philosophical in retrospect: 'I think my experience of working with Madonna was so valuable – I learned so much.'

The choice of new producer fell upon Reggie Lucas, a multi-talented musician who had been a sideman for Miles Davis before turning to record production and song-writing. Lucas had been a successful producer for Stephanie Mills, among others, before working with Madonna. The songs chosen were 'Burning Up', which was written by Madonna, and a number called 'Physical Attraction' composed by Reggie Lucas especially for her, which he wrote after seeing the video Steinberg had made of 'Everybody' and also after seeing Madonna in action on stage.

Her second single reveals the new producer's hand: the sound is fuller, and her voice is more fully integrated within the texture, especially in 'Physical Attraction', which was clearly written with no other singer in mind but her. The vocal line of 'Physical Attraction' is pitched slightly lower than in 'Everybody', which not only brings the naturally deeper qualities of Madonna's voice to the fore, but adds a new facet to her recorded timbre. But, like 'Everybody', the Lucas song is still dance-oriented in beat if not in message: on this track, Lucas adds a more solid beat track, fractionally behind the pulse, deeper but by no means hefty, which suits the lower pitch of the song perfectly.

'Burning Up', Madonna's own composition, takes the title very much as its starting point. Faster and funkier than 'Everybody', it jumps into life with sudden horror-chords, and Madonna's voice, when she enters, is more nasal in quality than before – surrounded with tightly phased echo, it also appears bigger.

Both sides of the new single clearly had hit potential and were given video treatment by Ed Steinberg. For 'Burning Up', the video features a car which tries to drive Madonna down: the driver of the vehicle was a painter, Kenny Compton, whom she was having a brief relationship with at the time but they split up almost immediately after making the video.

'Physical Attraction' was an even bigger dance hit than the first single, so at least no-one could now claim that Madonna was a one-off phenomenon. And, in addition, it was becoming clear that she possessed a new quality of overt feminine sexuality, which struck a ready response from both boys and girls: having it both ways, Madonna was becoming the personification of a boy's dreams as well as a modern-day role-model for liberated girls. This unique aspect of her appeal was something which would assume greater importance over the coming months and years.

And so, almost inevitably, an album was mooted, but her contract with Sire only called for three singles. The album option was invoked, and plans for this important project were set in train. However, it was not to be entirely plain sailing, for although Lucas had been engaged to produce it, and the album was to include her three previously released songs, the aim was to have the abortive 'Ain't No Big Deal' featured as the opening track. This number seems to have been jinxed: the version she had made with Mark Kamins had been disappointing and the new version produced by Reggie Lucas was equally unuseable.

As it transpired, the album – originally released and titled simply *Madonna*, but later reissued as *Madonna – The First Album* – opens with another song by Madonna, 'Lucky Star'. To those familiar with Reggie Lucas's productions on the previous two songs, this betokens his hallmark, but it begins with a fascinating synthesizer cascade up and down the keyboard before a solid (but not overpowering) rhythm sets the beat afoot based on a delicious bass riff, tight and moving in on itself. Madonna enters without more ado, the 'Lucky Star' being the boy at her side. Once again, Madonna takes her distinctive voice down to its lowest register, later on embroidering it with double-tracking in her higher, tighter timbre. The result is a cumulative, hypnotic opening number, towards the end of which the cascading synthesizers unfurl over her voice: an excellent first track, which does not entirely prepare us for the opening of the next number, 'Borderline', another song written especially for Madonna by Lucas.

Like a mixed glockenspiel-vibraphone creation, simple slow chords under a little tune usher the song gently in, a mild attention-getter before the drums fly into life as the tune brings Madonna to our attention. The beat is less subtle than in 'Lucky Star', and the texture a little too sweet-toothed for rock, but the aching urgent melody restores the balance. Now, as the introduction returns, the elements of 'Borderline' click into place as though they were clockwork, and this excellent pop-dance number surges to its conclusion, the fade being particularly brilliantly managed.

'Burning Up' is next, and is followed by 'I Know It', a sparkling atmosphere strangely at odds with the words, which, when read by themselves, do not suggest the music they are set to. For example: 'I don't know why I thought that I could make you happy/These tears I cry for you are so hopeless . . . And now I know you don't care . . .' – and so on in this vein. On the face of it, these lines seem to demand a suitably sad treatment. But this is Madonna, the 'So what?' girl, identifying the problem but telling us that it means little to her in the long run, especially as the unusual rising chords, half a step at a time, almost literally raise the spirits. This is more than a passable number but there is something faintly scrappy about the overall result, as though the song had not been fully thought through before the recording was made. It has some redeeming features: a dirty saxophone which breaks loose from time to time, for one, but there is an element of 'we'll-make-a-dance-track-out-of-this-no-matter-what' which devalues the production. Perhaps this is what Madonna meant when she said, of the album's progress in the studio, that she felt uncertain to express her opinions as to the way the production seemed to be going: most artists are a little in awe at first of the banks of technical equipment in control rooms, and in her case it was only when the album was about three-quarters through that she felt confident enough to voice her thoughts.

Be that as it may, her professionalism is shown at its finest in the next song, 'Holiday', which in vinyl and cassette formats begins side two. The failure of 'Ain't No Big Deal' to gel a second time in the studio led to the album being one song short: seven were ready when eight were needed. Also, it seems, the album was going over budget, and was still incomplete. Apparently Madonna herself was responsible for talking the powers-that-be into providing more money, but the replacement song came from an entirely new source.

The Warner Brothers disco promotion team had recently introduced Madonna to John 'Jellybean' Benitez, a well-known disc-jockey at the Funhouse discotheque, and they had quickly become lovers. He is a native of the South Bronx district, where street-wisdom was born, and recalls that 'I thought she had a lot of style, and she crossed over a lot of boundaries because everyone in the rock clubs played her – the black clubs, the gay, the straight; and very few records have that appeal.'

Jellybean's arrival in Madonna's life was significant: they hit it off personally almost immediately, and flirted a lot, especially in public. They soon went out together frequently, drawn by their physical attraction and their common aims and personalities. Madonna found him a great companion, and rather more than that: they enjoyed each other's company, during a relationship which lasted, on and off, for about two years. Jellybean is a star in his own right: signed to Chrysalis Records, he has released several important dance albums.

It was Jellybean who found the replacement song for Madonna's first album. In his capacity as disc-jockey, he was often handed demo-tapes of new material (as Madonna had herself done with Mark Kamins), and one which had caught his attention was 'Holiday', written by Curtis Hudson and Lisa Stevens. He played it to Madonna, who liked it immediately, and she managed to persuade

Sire that Jellybean should produce the song for her album. Both of them knew that a lot rested on their work, yet such was their preparation and dedication that they put the entire track down in one day.

As a consequence, Madonna's first album ended up with three producers being credited: it is unlikely that any other debut album of the time had such myriad production credits. 'Holiday' bears no signs of inexperience: on the contrary the opening, once heard, can never be forgotten – the soft adjacent chords, a perfect auditory equivalent of a still summer's day, above an insistent but gently equable pulse. An attractive descending scale, a scrap of a tune – no more – ushers Madonna in, almost with her 'Everybody' voice, calling out the words 'holiday' and 'celebrate' as in the near distance. The atmosphere is immediately appealing, the chords making a soft cushion for the simple song she sings, itself made up of small phrases at first, like ideas as they occur to a relaxed and calm mind. Eventually a piano enters, brilliantly played by Fred Zarr in jerkily honky-tonk style, flicking through the music as some siesta arabesque.

After this high-spot, 'Think of Me' can only come across in the nature of an anti-climax. It is possibly the weakest track on the album, although it has some redeeming features. Madonna's over-dubs are well handled and are among the best on the album, but overall the song fails to take wing: the message is essentially downbeat, about a girl warning her boyfriend that he's going to lose her if he doesn't treat her better, but is written to an upbeat setting, which even Bobby Malach's fine saxophone solo cannot entirely rescue.

'Physical Attraction' and 'Everybody' round out the album, which in some ways is an amazing piece of work overall. It is not, and cannot be, one of the greatest albums of all time, but it absolutely declares Madonna as an original artist of wide appeal. It avoids all pretence, or 'message', and is refreshingly free from the self-indulgence or sheer incompetence which so often mars debut albums. Madonna's first album is all there, and whilst one would never turn to it for intellectual stimulation, it was never so intended. What it has, and continues to have years later, is a genuine freshness and positive attitude to life which cannot but put the listener in a good mood. As we have seen, it is far from slapdash, and contains much which is purely musical and subtly original.

As it transpired, Madonna's first album was returned to in the future when newer remixed versions of various songs on it were made and issued. Like most albums which are successful, it came to mean a lot to the artist and personnel involved. For many of them, it was very much a leap forward into virgin territory. But perhaps the most touching aspect of all is the single line at the end of the album's credits: 'This album is dedicated to my father.'

It was released in the USA in July 1983, a month after Madonna's third single 'Holiday' had been issued. This was a reasonable hit, but was nonetheless something of a disappointment for both Warner Brothers and Madonna, for everyone had expected it to make a greater impact. But internationally her growing success and the album's investment made different propositions for Warner Brothers. WEA (Warner-Elektra-Atlantic) in London had high hopes for the album when the tapes arrived from America, and Madonna travelled to the UK for her first visit in the summer of 1983. It was essentially a visit to get the feel of London, to meet a few people and to do what she could to promote her work.

However, at that time few people in the pop media had heard of her (Madonna's releases in the UK had met with little response, with WEA passing on the first of her singles) and her appearance at the Camden Palace, when she mimed to her songs, went by hardly noticed. If she returned to America somewhat chastened by her first encounter with London there is no doubt that her experience had given her much food for thought: she knew exactly what she now had to do in order to conquer England.

In September and October of 1983 sales in the USA of her albums were encouraging without being outstanding, but as November approached, and with it Thanksgiving, radio stations across America began to pick up on 'Holiday'. The result was that Madonna's third single caught the public mood as she had never done before. Crossing all barriers, it started to sell in great quantities: at last, Warner Brothers had a hit on their hands – a big one.

An old adage in the record business, that 'if you have a chart single you have a chart album', was proved again in this instance: now, the perfect combination of the deal Madonna had done with

Sire came to fruition. Sire was a label small enough in staffing to give the artist daily personal attention, the kind of familial support which is virtually essential for a young career – what any artist needs, after all, is encouragement, preferably constant encouragement – and yet Warner Brothers were big enough, not only nationally but also internationally, to move into gear the instant a record looks like being a hit and to bring into play their vast resources of personnel in press and promotion, sales and marketing, to extract the maximum return from their consolidated efforts. In other words, almost without realizing it, and certainly without planning it, with Sire Madonna had it all ways.

By the end of 1983, therefore, with a massive hit and a fine debut album being much talked about and bought, Madonna could return home for Thanksgiving secure in the knowledge that she had achieved much of her ambition since she took the airplane to New York with thirty-five dollars seven years earlier. By whatever route she had travelled, she had made it. But there was more to do, and much more to achieve.

5

LIKE A VIRGIN

As 1984 dawned, Madonna was approaching the height of her initial
chart success. One thing was lacking to complete the equation –
exposure on the influential MTV network. Another single, 'Borderline', was taken from the first album early in the New Year and a
fine video was made for it, produced by Bruce Logan and Michele
Ferrone and directed by Mary Lambert. Displaying a remarkable
degree of sophistication and artistry compared to other videos
being made at the time, 'Borderline' features Madonna pursuing
a handsome, Hispanic-looking boy in a small town. As she becomes
famous, having modelled for a photo session and appeared on the
cover of *Gloss* magazine, he gets more interested until eventually
she is invited into the 'man's world' of the pool hall and the boy
is teaching her to play pool. The storyline shows her gaining more
control of her own life, to the point where she can refuse to wear the
floppy hat that the photographer wants her to wear. From being a
little girl with an orangey-red bow in her hair, she has become a
knowing woman who gets what she wants.

One week later, in February 1984, the video to 'Lucky Star'
was made. This was something different from the 'Borderline'
clip: a new team – Arthur Pierson directing, Glenn Goodwin the
producer – with Madonna as art director, took a song lasting a
full minute and ten seconds longer than 'Borderline' and proceeded
to make something infinitely less interesting visually out of it.
Basically it is just Madonna, with a boy and a girl, dancing
against a virginal white background, and features close-up shots
of Madonna's by now famous midriff. The dancing is good and
the song (mixed for the video by Jellybean) sounds fine, but the

overall effect quickly become monotonous and at five minutes is far too long.

Having seen her continuing chart success and the dynamic quality of the 'Borderline' video, however, MTV could no longer resist Madonna's blandishmental combination of hit records and outstandingly professional dancing, although the single 'Lucky Star' had to wait until 'Borderline' had exhausted its own full chart potential. For all the trials and tribulations which had attended its birth, Madonna's first album was turning into a veritable goldmine of chart material, and by the spring of 1984 it had been on the album charts continuously for nine months. At this point the media moved in, with Madonna undertaking a series of interviews for the press, radio and television. In the nature of things, not all of the interviews were sympathetic to her, but she was undoubtedly an entirely new kind of pop phenomenon; whatever her fans and detractors had read and heard about her, Madonna had almost literally starved to get where she was, and had certainly paid her dues.

Some of the articles at this time were to claim that Madonna had used the 'casting couch' method of achieving success, having affairs with any men who could help her in her career. This impression was fostered by her stage persona and videos and Madonna herself did not deny it, in fact on occasion she encouraged the rumours. She *had* worked with some of the men that she had relationships with – like Dan Gilroy and Jellybean. But there is no evidence that she slept with anyone influential at Sire Records; she certainly did not have an affair with George Lucas or Freddie De Mann; and there are various other people who could have been very useful to her that she chose not to jump into bed with. The truth is the other way round. As a dedicated musician her social circle consisted of musicians and their friends. She inevitably chose her lovers from this circle and once she was involved with a musician, what could be more natural than to work with him? As Jellybean said, 'She took advantage of the opportunities given – other people do the same thing.'

As a result of the success of the 'Borderline' single, the album was doing even more business and its chart position improved as each week passed. But when, in the summer of 1984, 'Lucky Star' was also released as a single and proceeded to follow 'Borderline' up the charts, it became the biggest-selling and fastest-climbing single she had ever had, sending the 'album sales through the roof', as Michael Rosenblatt commented. These album sales now crossed the magic platinum figure (in excess of one million units in the USA), and her international potential could no longer be ignored. She returned to Great Britain, where at last her records had begun to make some impact. 'Holiday' entered the UK charts in January 1984, and stayed there for a total of eleven weeks, eventually peaking at number 6, making it the first of Madonna's record-breaking British singles. In its wake, 'Lucky Star' had also begun to return good sales figures. During this British visit Madonna was seen on several television shows, notably on the BBC's influential 'Top of the Pops'. For the 'Holiday' chart appearances she wore a black vest, with another multi-coloured vest over black leggings cut off at the knee, a black skirt over top and black boots, grey socks and lots of bangles. However, once again she felt less than fully-understood by some sections of the British press, who were prone to describing her as 'an inexperienced tart [who had] struck lucky at her local disco'. *Smash Hits*' review of 'Borderline' must also have been disappointing to her: 'This weak effort is pretty borderline as a song and will be lucky if it borders on the charts. Will somebody please give this girl some real songs instead of excuses.'

But from the UK, Madonna remained in Europe, travelling to Italy for video location shots in Venice for a new song, 'Like A Virgin', the video of which was completed on 18 July. Curiously, her then-current single, 'Lucky Star', had originally been released in the UK in September 1983 (making it her second British single, following 'Everybody', which, on its first release, had not been successful), but initially it failed to make much impact. Warner Brothers persisted in their belief in the hit potential of the single, however, and re-released and re-promoted it in the wake of the success of 'Holiday'. 'Lucky Star' began to pick up healthy UK disco play until on 17 March 1984 it eventually entered the UK charts, reaching number 14 – the highest position it enjoyed during its nine weeks in the Top 75 – in May.

At the time of the peak sales for the UK single, Madonna had already recorded a track, 'Sidewalk Talk', for the EMI-America Records debut solo album by John 'Jellybean' Benitez, entitled *Wotupski!?!*, which had been released in May 1984. This track, which is probably heard to its best advantage as music on the extended dance mix version on the double-album *Jellybean Rocks the House*, where the singer is Catherine Buchanan, is a good example of Hispanic-dance early house music, with its images of Hispanic street life, the vocal line pattering conspiratorially between adjacent notes as if it were secret chatter amongst street-wise girls.

By the summer of 1984, Madonna had progressively developed into a very hot property for Sire/Warner Brothers, with enormous potential. The completion of a second album, on which she had intermittently been working since the beginning of the year, now became something of an urgent consideration. After all, even though her initial album had supplied a series of major hit singles, some of the tracks on that first album were almost two years old. Madonna had not only come a long way since the launch of her debut album but had also had a lot of new ideas for songs which could be realized on a second album. In addition, the nature of her success, which was now transcontinental, meant that she could command the finest production staff then available. With 'Like A Virgin', she had already commenced work on it.

During the summer of 1984 the second album had taken concrete form with the engagement of the internationally respected producer and musician Nile Rodgers to oversee it. Perhaps in view of the ongoing triumph of the first album, Reggie Lucas had not unnaturally imagined that he would be asked to produce the second, but Madonna was still unconvinced that her talents had been as well projected during those sessions as they might, for all the songs' subsequent successes. Nile Rodgers' reputation stemmed from the fact that during the previous year he had produced David Bowie's first EMI (American Capitol) album, *Let's Dance*, in New York. When it was released it soon became the fastest-selling album EMI had had since the Beatles' *Sergeant Pepper* sixteen years previously, the title track staying at number one in the UK singles charts for over a month. (Bowie's two succeeding singles, 'China Girl' and 'Modern Love', also from the Rodgers-produced album, both got to number two.) Nile Rodgers had also just produced the highly successful and deeply impressive Paul Simon solo album, *Hearts and Bones*, in addition to one of Duran Duran's biggest hits, 'Wild Boys'.

So the choice of Nile Rodgers was a brilliant move and something of a coup: good though the first album had been, before ten seconds of the start of the second album (which was finished at the end of July) have elapsed we know that we are in a different world. Yet the album's release was delayed owing to the on-going success of the 'Lucky Star' single in the USA and the ever-increasing success of the album from which it was taken. A pre-release glimpse of 'Like A Virgin' caused a sensation when Madonna performed it live at that year's MTV Awards ceremony, creating an immense interest in the as-yet-unavailable recording. Dedicated, more cryptically than the first, 'To the virgins of the world' (although the sepia-style cover photographs show Madonna as anything but one herself), this second album is named *Like A Virgin*, after the title of the third song it contains, and the first to be recorded.

As if to compensate Reggie Lucas for being passed over as producer for the second album, he did finally see the release of the abortive song from the first album, 'Ain't No Big Deal', on an American Warner Brothers' compilation album *Revenge of the Killer Bs* volume 2, where Madonna's performance of the Steve Bray song can be found, given somewhat less than star billing, on side 2, band 5. One should not be hard on Lucas: his work on Madonna's initial album was by no means unsatisfactory so far as the public was concerned, but the influence and control of Nile Rodgers are apparent from the very beginning as the different world of the new album bursts into life with 'Material Girl'.

Tony Thompson's tenor-drum-up-beat thwack sets a tremendous dance rhythm into focus, the main pulse coming on the second beat of the bar, against which Bernard Edwards' bass follows the rhythm like a cat: this is a Nile Rodgers production, and no mistake. The ambience is set in a fatter acoustic than that in which we have heard Madonna previously, one which shows allegiance both to dance and garage-music. However, this texture is aimed less at dance-floor giant loudspeakers, where a tighter sound is needed: most dance venues are poor acoustically, and as records are always played there at full volume, a fat recorded sound will be destroyed – sounding even fatter, and losing the detail. The best dance-style records pare the sound almost to the bone. Rodgers's ability to judge this fatter yet by no means obfuscating acoustic to perfection is one of his greatest assets.

Madonna, as recorded here, has a much fuller voice than we might have expected, but it suits the material in more ways than one. The message is almost entirely loveless: a yuppie message long before yuppies came and went, and one which neatly turns the traditional boy-girl relationship on its head. The song, by Peter Brown and Robert Rans, is not particularly subtle, but it contains genuinely musical subtleties nonetheless, the harmonies changing slowly whilst the tune barely moves its tonal base. As the words convey, Madonna is very much a material girl here, only interested in boys with money (''Cause the boy with the cold hard cash/Is always Mister Right'), and treating them merely as meal-tickets or as playthings. There is a reason for this, a prevalent attitude: '. . . we're living in a material world, And I am a material girl'. In fact, the song is a satire of Reaganomics and the materialistic attitudes they fostered, but many people didn't get this point.

The accompanying video is a recreation of the scene in the film *Gentleman Prefer Blondes* when Marilyn Monroe sang 'Diamonds Are A Girl's Best Friend', with Madonna dressed as Marilyn in shoulderless dress and elbow-length gloves. The choreography is also the same, right down to the arms thrust high to reveal the armpits that became a classic Monroe trademark. This is no piece of nostalgia, however, although we know that Madonna was a fan of Monroe's. Rather, the juxtaposition of the soft, feminine Monroe image with the mechanical sound of 'Material Girl' demonstrates the difference between the two women, even if their lyrics had the same message. Monroe was ultimately destroyed by men's attitudes to her sexuality back in the 1950s; Madonna is in charge of the situation and using sex to get men exactly where she wants them. 'She was a victim, I'm not' is how Madonna succinctly put it.

'Angel', the second song on *Like A Virgin*, is a fast-paced disco number written by Madonna and Steve Bray. It is a love song but not in the generally accepted sense of the phrase, for the Linn and Simmons drum machine programming will not let it get at all serious. Nor will Madonna, for the first we hear of her is her attractive soft laughter, falling down the scale. This mixture of romantic serious lyrics with cheerful upbeat music had already become a Madonna hallmark, which seems to imply 'Don't take things too seriously.'

'Like A Virgin' itself follows, more medium-paced than the predecessor. The lyrics are full of classic Madonna double entendres, such as 'Your love thawed out what was scared and cold' and 'Feels so good inside when you hold me' and the deliberately provocative message that she feels like a virgin again since meeting this new guy made great copy for the newspapers in conjunction with the name 'Madonna'. The 'Like A Virgin' video, shot in Venice, is visually very beautiful, with Madonna in a white wedding dress, and a lion prowling the streets. The man wears a lion-mask (man as predator) and grabs her to whisk her off in a gondola. Both surreal and startling in places, it is the photography of the Venetian canals and buildings that stands out in this video.

'Over and Over', the fourth song on side one, was also written by Madonna and Steve Bray and is a nicely-paced, medium-tempo Hispanic soft-beat number, with the message that in spite of life's knocks, one gets up again 'over and over'. Nile Rodgers exactly reinforces this message by having Madonna's voice echoing and re-echoing ('over and over'), making it fly away in the distance and disappear from our perception.

Good though all the songs on the first side are, there can be little argument that the final song, 'Love Don't Live Here Anymore', written in 1978 by Miles Gregory, is musically the most outstanding of the five. It comes as a complete contrast to those which have preceded it; Nile Rodgers seems to have profoundly understood the true nature of this song, for he gives it a symphonic arrangement, with a large string section conducted by himself, not imitated by banks of synthesizers – which are deployed on this track in other ways. Madonna's performance is masterly, with excellent breath-control and appropriate and moving injunctions, confounding those critics who had claimed that she couldn't sing.

'Dress You Up', written by Peggy Stanziale and Andrea LaRusso, opened side two on the original version of the album but 'Into the Groove' was added subsequently at this point. Those who bought the original version of the album will have first heard the four sharp tenor-drum beats prior to the disco rhythm which underlines 'Dress You Up'. In some ways, this song bears a superficial resemblance to 'Over and Over'; 'Dress You Up' is a song of admiration by the girl for the boy, and is vocally in two parts: in the first, she sings a sinuous theme, like a girl softly running her hands over a man's naked body; in the second, a faster hook line in double-time, the line is higher.

Madonna wrote the next song, 'Shoo-Bee-Doo', and begins it

straightaway, without preamble. It is a slow, gently-paced number, with delicate piano filigree trailing behind her voice as she explains her confusion to her man: 'when I look in your eyes . . . I see so much confusion and it's killing me'. He is close to tears over a previous affair ('I can see you've been hurt before, but don't compare them to me'). She attempts to console him with baby-talk, bringing to mind a reference on the album's inner sleeve: 'Jellybean, Goo Goo Ga Ga'.

'Pretender', which follows, is another Madonna-Steve Bray number, a hurt and aggressive-sounding song in which Madonna, in close harmony with her backing singers, warns other girls not to fall for the pretender's charms. The final song is 'Stay', yet another Madonna-Steve Bray composition, whose character is more humorous than its predecessor, starting more funkily in rhythm with a constant triplet pulse behind each beat. The song is a good one, as we might expect by now from this team, but it is not completely outstanding. It has all the right ingredients, but it gives the impression of having had too many cooks attending at the preparation of the broth. Being a fair pop song of its type, it is also a good party-disco number, even though it lacks the qualities which would turn it into a really distinctive hit. At the end, Madonna's repeated 'Love Me's' are the last sounds we hear: a far cry from the material girl with which the album opened. This is the true 'message' of the album, if you like: that love and human relationships are the valuable things in life and not vast quantities of money.

And thus does this superb album end. Madonna has appeared not just to have been supremely self-confident throughout, but has demonstrated to all that she possesses a surprisingly wide sympathy with varied material, and was more fully produced than before – perhaps, in a phrase, more glamorously presented – to the extent that as this album closes one can fearlessly state that Madonna had definitively arrived. The material and the sound are of excellent quality throughout and the entire album concept is both original and well carried through. No wonder, therefore, that the people at Sire and Warner Brothers were highly excited when the tapes were first played to them.

It is customary in the record business for new albums by important artists to be released towards the end of the year, in what is generally accepted as the big buying season when the companies' salesmen do their deals with the retailers stocking up for the usual Christmas rush. By the time that the 1984 main-selling season came upon the record company, Madonna had grown into an even bigger star than she had been when the album was first mooted at the beginning of the year. In addition, the delay in releasing it meant that a more detailed and extensive marketing plan, including outlets which might not have been so receptive earlier, could be put together. The result was spectacular: the immediate success of the *Like A Virgin* album, elbowing most of the new records from other big acts down the charts. It is one thing for a passable album by an established singer or group to get into the charts, but quite another, in the case of the release of Madonna's second album at the end of 1984, for it to have exceeded the aspirations of her new-found millions of fans throughout the world, in the process capping the unhoped-for expectations of the first album with substantially greater sales within a shorter period of time.

6

FILMING AND TOURING

By the time of the eventual release of the *Like A Virgin* album in November 1984, Madonna's career was spectacularly poised. The new album was eagerly awaited by both public and the trade, and a superb video had been made to promote the title track as her new single. Her face adorned almost as many posters and T-shirts as James Dean's or Marilyn Monroe's. The massive chart success she had enjoyed had made her virtually a household name, and it was known that she was anxious to prove her worth as an actress.

To this end, she signed up with the well-known William Morris Agency who had succeeded in obtaining offers for her for a number of films: not starring roles, of course, but smaller supporting or cameo appearances in order to gain valuable experience. However, comparatively unknown and inexperienced actors and actresses have to audition, as do more established artists: Madonna auditioned for several roles, including a part in the Herbert Ross film *Footloose*, which was made at the end of 1984, but she was not selected for the part. The film attempted, not entirely successfully, to emulate the previous year's surprise hit, *Flashdance*. One of the stars of *Footloose* was a young Californian actor named Christopher Penn. Madonna knew of him vaguely already because her song 'Burning Up' had been used as a background to a scene in his 1984-released movie *The Wild Life*.

But two far more significant events followed quite quickly. Firstly, she was offered a small part as a nightclub singer in the Jon Peters production *Vision Quest* (the title was changed to *Crazy for You* when the film was eventually released in Britain). Madonna described it as 'a coming-of-age movie about a guy who's training for the Olympics.

In the end he wins his big fight but loses his girl.' Madonna's part in this was 'not exactly an acting role, but it was a bona fide movie, and it was an invaluable foot in the door.' She had been asked to provide three songs for the soundtrack, but in the event only 'Gambler,' written by her, and 'Crazy for You', by John Bettis and Jon Lind, were used. Both were produced by Jellybean, with whom Madonna was then living in Soho, where they had recently moved into a much larger apartment.

Although Madonna's part in the movie was small, her impact was out of all proportion to her role: by the time of the release of the film in December 1984, she had become a major attraction. For a star of her magnitude to have condescended to appear in a cameo role represented a major coup by the production company and it was because of her impact that the title was changed to *Crazy for You* when it was released in Britain in February 1985. Footage from the film in which Madonna appears was issued later in the year as a commercial video release.

If so much had come from such a comparatively minor screen appearance, the second event was of far greater importance. This was a starring role in the comedy *Desperately Seeking Susan*, which had been cast in the summer of 1984, not without some misgivings on the part of some of the Orion moguls who felt then that Madonna's comparative inexperience made her casting a risky proposition. But the film was not a substantial investment, Madonna was not the star, and the director Susan Seidelman preferred her to the almost two hundred other applicants for the part.

Madonna appeared at the audition, as Susan Seidelman has said, 'nervous and vulnerable and not at all arrogant. Sweet, but intelligent and verbal, with a sense of humour.' Within a little while, Seidelman 'just started seeing her as Susan. She has the kind of face you want to look at blown up fifty feet; she isn't conventionally beautiful but then neither were Bette Davis or Marlene Dietrich. I didn't choose her because she was a rock star, I'm interested in interesting people.'

As it transpired, Madonna's extraordinary string of luck continued with her landing the part of Susan. At the time, she secured the part on her own merits and appeal; but had the film been cast a year later her chart success would have ensured that she would have been too expensive a property to consider for such a comparatively low-budget venture. As a profile of Madonna in *Time* magazine for 27 May 1985 pointed out, *Desperately Seeking Susan* brought her a new audience for her talents – the film and video market. And by the time of the release of the film, Madonna's impact with the *Like A Virgin* album and single ensured good box-office business.

This whole combination of publicity could not have been better but it would have meant nothing for the success of the film if Madonna's performance had been less than good. The character she plays, Susan, is a free spirit – running away from commitments, completely individual in her style of dress and in her mode of living, staying at one boyfriend's apartment for a while and then moving on to another without leaving a forwarding address, dancing the night away at the wildest clubs and breaking men's hearts along the way. This is exactly the character that Madonna was coming to represent for her fans – fast-living, whacky and, above all, free to do her own thing. This was a particularly appealing image for the teenage fans still trapped within parental restraints.

As if to underline the similarities between Susan and Madonna, she is often seen in the film wearing an outfit with the initials 'M.C.' emblazoned on the top. In the context of the film this stood for 'Magic Club', but they are also Madonna's own initials. And the nightclub scene was shot at 30 West 21st Street – the address of the Danceteria where Madonna first met Mark Kamins, who was instrumental in getting her signed to Sire Records.

Certainly there were real similarities between Susan and Madonna, but the main difference was that while the former floats around seemingly unemployed, the latter was a workaholic who drove herself hard and was committed to succeeding in life. She was already coming to be seen by her many fans – and this film added to them – as a symbol of the 1980s cult of the individual. She did not stand for any group in society and could not be categorized. She was not just a 'disco singer' or a 'pop artist', a 'femme fatale' or a 'tart'. She was a conglomerate, a one-off, unique in her mixture of talents and the dedication she applied to each.

The story of *Desperately Seeking Susan* is that of a bored housewife, played by Rosanna Arquette, who loves reading the small ads in the personal columns of the newspapers. She is fascinated by a series of ads featuring the character 'Susan' and she imagines the exciting life this Susan must lead. Finally an ad appears asking Susan to come to a meeting and naming the time and the place so she decides to turn up and see what this Susan is like. There is an accident, Rosanna Arquette's character loses her memory and is mistaken for Susan, then, by a series of humorous coincidences, the two women swap lives for a while – the old prince and the pauper theme with a new twist. The film is variously a comedy, a mystery story and a romance, light and ultimately insubstantial but nevertheless made interesting by the performances of the two women.

The success of *Desperately Seeking Susan* took many people – especially the critics – completely by surprise. It hit the Madonna-youth market exactly and became the fifth-biggest-earning film in the USA in 1985, making a substantial return of over forty million dollars in the USA alone for Orion's comparatively small outlay. The film also did wonders for both girls' careers: Rosanna Arquette received a British Film Academy Award for her portrayal, although her relationship with Madonna on and off the set caused a few raised eyebrows.

When the film was cast, it was Rosanna Arquette who had the greater claim to fame as an actress: she also had top billing. But by the time the shooting had commenced, and the nine weeks set aside for making the film had got under way, she began to feel as though Madonna had taken over. Madonna was then enjoying great chart success, and it was Madonna whom the public was more and more eager to read about and to want to see on their screens. Rosanna commented, 'I thought I was going to be making this small, charming film, not some rock video.' The film is both small (104 minutes originally; 99 minutes in the video version) and fairly charming, and there is some substance to Ms Arquette's claim of feeling that she was taking part in a rock video.

Perhaps her feelings were exacerbated when she learned that Susan Seidelman had asked Madonna – very much a decision made spontaneously and late in the film's planning, after shooting had commenced – to write a song to be featured in the film. This was no 'title-song', a potential chart success by a well-known artist, the kind of additional promotion which would accrue fame to the film: the series of James Bond films perhaps is the best-known example of this use of popular music. Seidelman saw Madonna's song as germane to the film's argument and not inappropriate to the character of Susan. As such, this was a very different proposition, genuinely made and valid in itself, and an opportunity which Madonna seized with alacrity.

Madonna and Steve Bray immediately went off to write a song and made a demonstration tape of it that they presented to Seidelman. It was exactly what she had in mind and the tape was of such good quality that she decided to use it straight on the soundtrack, without getting Madonna to re-record it under normal studio conditions.

'Into The Groove' – which is heard complete over the closing credits – is not the only music in the film: songs by Aretha Franklin, Iggy Pop, Dee Dee Sharp, Run DMC, Carly Simon and The Fixx, among others, enhance the soundtrack, and it says a great deal for Madonna's ability that her contribution stands up well in such company.

After the film was released, there was a great public demand to buy copies of Madonna's song, to the extent that Sire and Warner Brothers decided to add this number, which was called 'Into The Groove', to the recently released *Like A Virgin* album, where it now begins side two in the vinyl and cassette formats.

'Into The Groove' is a splendid song, with a freshness about it which displays the fact that it was written and performed straight off without endless studio revisions. It exhibits most of Madonna and Steve Bray's compositional fingerprints: a florid and continu-ously syncopated bass line, the use of adjacent chords to impart a bitter-sweet tension to the harmony, and a melody-line which often jumps by a series of thirds – in other words, most often based on the notes of the basic chord, which, with the blurred harmony, will often set Madonna's voice off against the urgent and uncertain background. Few of their songs have shown these characteristics to quite the same integrated degree as does 'Into The Groove'; as it begins, the catchy bass-line rhythm is very important – it is infectious and insistent, almost demanding by itself that everyone gets up to dance. Madonna's voice is lighter than we usually hear (if one plays this song as part of the *Like A Virgin* album, which it subsequently became, the difference in her vocal timbre is made clear). In addition, the voice has been treated with echo at all times, yet it is clear that her actual vocal quality was quite closely miked during the take. The result is a much tighter and more appropriately dance-like atmosphere which acts as a unifying agent throughout the song. It is a remarkably effective recording, and proof of the high standard of accomplishment then reached by Madonna and by Steve Bray, since few first-shot demonstration tapes are good enough to be considered for commercial release.

In spite of the success of the film, the making of it was not quite the fun time that Madonna fondly imagined it might be. She found the interminable amount of time just sitting around whilst the technicians made sure everything was just right for the next shot to be, as she said, 'a real drag . . . it drove me crazy'. But however much she may have felt impatience and nervousness – 'I was so nervous I opened my mouth and nothing came out' – she impressed her colleagues by appearing at all times calm and collected. She would often be up at around 4.30 each morning, preparing herself for the day's shooting; she would arrive early on the set, and rehearse her lines assiduously, as well as take a keen interest in the technical side of film-making, becoming friendly with several members of the crew.

Madonna has always retained a great affection for *Desperately Seeking Susan*. She described the film, once it had been completed, as 'like a return to the simple caper comedies Claudette Colbert and Carole Lombard made in the thirties. They give you a taste of real life, some poignance, and leave you feeling up at the end.'

Now, with two hit albums, nine singles and a successful film under her belt, the fans were crying out to see Madonna live. This would be the major test. It's one thing putting together a snappy disco number in a studio with all modern technology at hand and the possibility of countless retakes if you get it wrong. But could Madonna sing live? If it was the technology of Steve Bray's portable studio which created the Madonna sound, or Nile Rodgers's more sophisticated creativity within the recording studio, then the audience would expect to hear those sounds in the auditorium.

It is by no means unusual for a present-day tour to be rehearsed for several months in advance. Concerts today are no longer merely a succession of songs: they are spectacles, a mixture of music, film and theatre at the centre of which is the artist.

The artist has to be centre-stage and readily identifiable. This would not be much of a problem if several spotlights were used, as used to be the case; but today, thanks to more compact microphones and the natural desire of artists to move on stage, spotlighting is not a reliable nor a continuous option. So in the 1980s tours have become

Previous page, A young Madonna with all of the fervour and professionalism of her later years. *Left,* Attired in a fashionable belted man's shirt, Madonna is soulful at a pre-success gig. *Below,* The heavy make-up and dark, cropped hair were her first 'look', as indicated by this early publicity shot.

Right, Madonna leaves LA airport on her way to Seattle for the first concert date of her 1985 tour. *Below,* Madonna Louise Ciccone: the look that captured the imagination of the world.

Above, Madonna with producer/TV show host Dick Clark at the American music awards in 1985. *Below,* Madonna and longtime boyfriend 'Jellybean' Benitez.

Left, Madonna grins cheekily as she poses for photographers at the 1985 American music awards. *Below,* Tousled and sultry, Madonna's sex-symbol image attracted men and women alike.

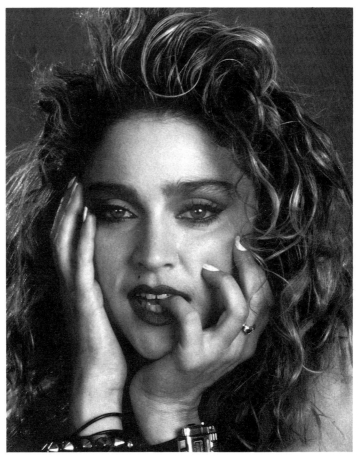

Right, Avoiding the ever-present paparazzi, Madonna leaves Koala Blue — a shop owned by Olivia Newton-John — in West Hollywood. *Below,* Joan Ciccone, Madonna's stepmother.

Above, Paula Ciccone, Madonna's younger sister. *Below,* Madonna and her designer brother Christopher arrive at the 'Joseph' fashion show in the US.

Above, Live Aid performers: Madonna is accompanied by the Rolling Stones, Hall and Oates, Bob Dylan and Tina Turner. *Below,* Bejewelled and sensuous, Madonna with the bangles and beads that created her first public image.

more and more about the artist's image and it is this image which informs the whole nature of each concert. Image has been with popular music for many decades, and its importance has been recognized long before the modern-day mega-tour was thought of. David Bowie was the first artist in the early 1970s consciously to create and discard images – from Ziggy Stardust to the 'Young American' soulman, and from the cold, clinical atmosphere of the *Station to Station* tour to the warm liveliness of the *Let's Dance* one. Image is created by the style of the music, the clothes the artist chooses to wear and their performance on stage, as well as the choice of sets and lighting. It is propagated through magazine or newspaper articles, radio and television interviews. Children's television is becoming an increasingly popular medium for record companies to promote current singles, alongside all the vocal music programmes. The modern-day tour will often have a generic title, probably that of the artist's most recent album, the songs from which will form the major part of the show, and it will engender myriad spin-offs: fashion and merchandizing in the form of ephemeral paraphernalia, T-shirts, pictures, 'souvenir' programmes, all forms of bits and pieces, the rights to use the artist's features often generating as much revenue as ticket-sales or album sales at the venue on the night. None of this can happen, however, if the image has not been decided upon before; for the necessary photographs have to be taken, and the merchandized material manufactured.

From what they had already seen of Madonna on video, audiences were going to expect a high standard of visual presentation and a sophisticated display of dancing, so everything had to be scrupulously prepared and rehearsed. Pat Leonard had been chosen as the musical director of the *Like A Virgin* tour. Initially he had refused the position but Madonna managed to persuade him to change his mind and when they got down to work they hit it off immediately. In fact, they worked so well together that before long Madonna had proposed that they worked together on writing future songs.

Madonna had been home to Rochester for Thanksgiving in November 1984 and she had asked her younger brother Christopher – already a talented designer – to take charge of her personal wardrobe for the tour, as well as the clothes for the dancers and the backing band. He did not design all the costumes himself, but supervised the overall result, and he arranged to have a small tent erected just behind the stage where his sister could quickly make costume changes.

The might of Warner Brothers was the other essential ingredient in setting up the *Like A Virgin* tour, which opened at the Paramount Theater in Seattle, Washington state, in April 1985 and encompassed 38 performances in 27 cities in the USA and one – Toronto – in Canada. Over 355,000 paying customers turned out to see her. Her on-going chart success was exceptional; by the time the *Virgin* tour began, Madonna had had four top ten singles since the beginning of the year in America alone – 'Like A Virgin', 'Crazy for You' and 'The Gambler' (both from the film *Vision Quest*, released in February, the same month that the soundtrack album was released on the Geffen label) and 'Into the Groove' from *Desperately Seeking Susan*. The amazing thing was that none of the last three hit singles was planned: they all came from films, and it was not until 'Material Girl' was released as a single that she had the second consecutive hit from the new album.

The ticket sales for every one of the venues set new records for the fastest sell-outs. Within two hours of them going on sale, every ticket had been sold: in New York City alone, where three concerts had been scheduled for dates in June at Radio City Music Hall in Manhattan, every one of the 17,622 tickets was sold within an astonishing 34 minutes – no other artist had sold out quicker. With a current top-grossing film, and not having been out of the singles charts, or the press, that year, the news of Madonna's first concert could not have been better timed.

The controversial Beastie Boys – with their violent, shouting, raunch-rock sound – were chosen to open the show and, as the tour progressed, they managed to attract a lot of adverse publicity. Still, it was all publicity. They remember the experience: 'She's really cool. We knew her when she was just famous in New York and on her '85 tour she asked us to support her for a week as a trial. In the first week she realized we were the perfect group because the audience hated us so much that by the time she went on stage they went crazy. We used to sneak out with her all the time from the hotel – she had to escape all these lawyers and people – and she'd dress up in crazy outfits like green wigs so no one would recognize her and buy us all drinks so we'd get really drunk and have a really good time.'

The Beastie Boys went on stage at 8 p.m. and, exactly an hour later, the lights dimmed for the start of Madonna's long-awaited set. An image of Madonna appeared, slide-projected onto gigantic screens set to the rear of the band. The drums flicked, the synthesizers cascaded, the chords and the slinky rhythms rebounded throughout the auditorium as 'Dress You Up' started the show. The audience naturally craned forward, looking for her, and immediately it was her silhouette, an arm raised upwards, which dominated the centre-screen. The screen gradually rose to reveal the girl herself, with her two hunky male dancers, Michael Perea (a New York boy) and Lyndon B. Johnson (from Los Angeles, known as 'Elbee'), one on each arm, atop the wide central stairs, which they provocatively walked down, a wide grin on her face, to the main stage itself.

Her clothes were a kaleidoscope of fashion, a riot of colour: a jacket of blue-green wove with a myriad large-Paisley-based pattern in orange, white, yellow, purple and green. Underneath she wore a purple lace brassiere with a wide open pattern encompassing each breast; this was echoed in her tights, stretching up to her diaphragm, and made from the same material as the brassiere, over which Madonna wore a blue-green mini skirt, a tiny coloured-studded belt around her hips, fingerless gloves, from the same material as the brassiere and tights and genuine short lace-up black boots. Her hair was wild and streaked and through it ran a long bow-tied ribbon-band. Her outfit was completed by a cascade of fashion jewellery round her neck and many bracelets on her wrists. 'Dress You Up' was the choice for the opening number, a love song to a man but here transformed also into love for the audience, and she began with a lightly brilliant series of dance steps like a great virtuoso warming up before getting down to the real thing.

The song segued into 'Holiday' – a hit now throughout the world. This really gave her a chance to show her dancing ability, the men supportive rather than threatening, all happiness and good-time, the Madonna look-alikes singing along as though she was each one of them, their heads shaking on the 'Holiday' four-note phrase. Now the third number, the one they all knew backwards, for it was 'Into The Groove' from *Desperately Seeking Susan*. They had all seen the film, the single was high in the charts, and Madonna moved suggestively around Michael and Elbee, raising the temperature the while, as the 'groove' can now mean whatever you want it to mean. In some concerts, she followed this with 'Everybody'.

At this point, Madonna disappeared offstage for the first costume change, leaving the band to jam over the adjacent chords of the last song and the riffs it contained before segueing into the beginning of 'The Gambler' (from *Vision Quest*). Suddenly, Madonna returned clutching a big portable stereo box – like most kids have – which she used with some none too subtle double-entendres. 'Every lady has a box', Madonna claimed, 'and my box is special, because it makes music. But it has to be turned on.' Now, she is the gambler personified, dressed all in black, skin-tight, skin-showing, raunchy and hot, using upright stage props to make the meaning clearer. Here the female gambler was seemingly taking risks – worlds away from the fun-girl of fifteen minutes earlier – as she leapt down to the stage and lay flat on her back, panting, momentarily in another world with the eyes shut fast behind dark glasses.

The audience stared: then she turned to look at them and began 'Borderline' – in some concerts 'Lucky Star' was sung at this point – and the atmosphere, previously intense and sensual, was now paradoxically lightened. Swinging round, and on her feet, the mood of the new song reduced the tension, but she had now taken off her top and more of her body could be seen; in the middle of the short revealing top was a clear large cut-out crucifix. Madonna was joined by Elbee and Michael – both wearing masculine versions of her tight clothing, with Madonna's black-tasselled-gloved hands firmly grasping a free-moving independent microphone.

The tempo slowed for 'Crazy for You' a song well-known to everyone in the audience since it had been a number one in America (it got to number two in the UK in June 1985). 'Angel' followed immediately and hundreds of big white balloons fell from the high ceiling on to the audience, who reached up to catch them. Printed on each balloon was the phrase 'Dreams Come True', and at the moment of contact between the audience and the balloons Madonna had everyone there, liking it or not, utterly and completely with her. Next she moved into 'Over and Over', the concluding 'shout it!s cascading over and over each other. Then immediately she moved into 'Burning Up', the high-spot and finale of the bigger second section of the show, the section of sexual implications, of risky wantonness and of coy intoxication. The stage was flooded with orange-red lights, Madonna was flat on her back again, the back of her head towards the audience, atop a small wide platform, reaching out and upwards towards her guitarist, James Harrah, who had detached himself from the band and was standing over her, reaching down to meet her supplications. Pinky-red smoke oozed into the atmosphere, getting more dense by the second until it enveloped both Madonna and the guitarist in great folds of mysterious fog as the song ended and the lights faded.

There was silence. Then suddenly, Madonna appeared again, blindingly lit as the white virgin in a stylized bridal outfit, her midriff still uncovered (as it had been throughout), her yards of veil making a curious visual complement to the red smoky haze which had just ended the previous section of the show, as she was carried to the stage by the hunky disco-kings. The mood now reverted to the fun-time of the opening: a few bars from Michael Jackson's 'Beat It' were thrown in, surely a public acknowledgement of the young master's influence on her, and then, set down on stage by her boy-toys, she called out 'You don't really think I'm a material girl, do you?' They all called back 'Yes' and she led into 'Material Girl', the concert's climax, at the end of which she pulled a vast wad of 'Madonna money' from her top and flung it far into the crowd: 'Take it,' she cried, 'it's caused me nothing but trouble!'

It seems as though the concert is over but as she was leaving the stage, a stern voice called to her: 'Madonna, get off that stage now!' 'But, Daddy, do I have to? I'm having so much fun.' 'Get off this instant, do you hear me, young lady?' 'Oh, all right, but at least let me get my fur.' Her fur wrap has been left on stage, on a mike stand. She comes back for it, her face transfixed with her wide and generous grin, and receives the ovation from the wildly yelling crowd. In Detroit, Tony Ciccone himself came on stage to drag his daughter off – an obvious sign of his acceptance of her chosen career.

The tour was sold out, the public went away well satisfied with what they had seen, and the show itself was a non-stop spectacle built around a succession of recent top ten singles by the artist herself, yet for some reason the press was by no means universally enthusiastic. She herself tended to dismiss unfavourable notices by claiming that 'I get out there and work. My fans love it, and they come from a wide age range, and all kinds of backgrounds. If they're happy, I'm happy – so much for all the goofs who want to decide if my show deserves an R or an X rating.' American newspapers are traditionally reactionary: the overwhelming majority of their readers are over the age of thirty and it is difficult – if not impossible – to find one writer on a city's leading newspaper who would risk incurring the wrath of the paper's owner by praising someone who seemed to be inciting the kids to kick over the traces. This is nothing new in popular music, but almost a Pavlovian reaction on the part of many weather-eye journalists.

As the show finished and the thousands in the audience trooped out into the night, what had they witnessed? What 'image' of Madonna had they seen, and what impact did it have on them? In the first set she was a saucy, devil-may-care rebel, wearing lingerie, brilliant colours, and masses of jewellery, including crucifixes. The 'gambler' outfit was much more explicitly sexy and daring, challenging girls to be seductive and men to be seduced. And the chaste, stereotyped bridal costume for 'Like A Virgin' appears to be poking fun at marriage while the lyrics of the song actually affirm the value of true love. The message to the girls appeared to be that of personal freedom: live your life, Madonna seemed to be saying, do your own thing, but never forget the fact that you are feminine, and use your femininity to get what you want. Love is important and sex is great fun. In some ways, the impact of this approach was the stronger because it mirrored herself. She was living proof of the success of such an approach, at a time before the ravaged economies of the western world had recovered from the downwave of the 1970s, and the final touch in the show – the 'father image' telling his little girl effectively to come home on time, stop playing around, and get upstairs to bed – would have mirrored exactly the daily lives of the girls in the audience themselves. Here was the personification of their own problems – and what also seemed a valid solution to them.

They all wanted to look like Madonna: this was the image and this was something they could create and recreate as often as they liked, thanks to the powerfully effective merchandizing which accompanied each date. The tour grossed over six million dollars – a million dollars a week – and, after the fifth concert, in San Francisco, broke merchandizing sales at all subsequent venues. There was, as is by now usual, a wide variety of merchandizing material on offer: T-shirts, sweat-shirts, jumpers, pictures, cards, posters, Madonna crucifix earrings, plastic bangles and rosaries, and so on – the customary paraphernalia which attends concerts. Any one of these items would have made it easy for those who decided they wanted to be like Madonna – those who soon came to be called the 'wannabes' – and to copy her styles.

There is a shop (Maripolitan) on Bleecker Street, Greenwich Village, owned by Maripol, a French designer who designed costumes for the Virgin Tour as well as the jackets in *Desperately Seeking Susan*, and one floor of this shop is devoted to Madonna. It's called 'Madonnaland'. In 1985 Madonna launched a clothes line called Yazoo, just when her punk chic image took off. She designed a series of Madonna concoctions, which took off in the trade. All were limited editions and nothing has been issued since.

When asked about her attitude to clothes, Madonna replied: 'I like to combine things but in a humorous way, like a uniform skirt and fishnets. I love dresses like Marilyn Monroe wore, those '50s dresses that were really tailored to fit a voluptuous body. A lot of stuff made now is for an androgynous figure, and it doesn't look good on me.'

Madonna seemed to be completely in charge of her own life and perhaps, the wannabes felt if they imitated her then they could get what they wanted as well. In fact, by this stage of her career Madonna really was in charge. She had personally supervised all the preparations for the tour and had deliberately kept it to a manageable size. The total crew was only thirty-six and just three large trucks carried the equipment. Private aircraft were out; instead they travelled on scheduled flights or interstate buses, maintaining the feeling amongst those taking part that they were all part of a team with no-one being treated differently than anyone else. Madonna just had one bodyguard – a burly 20-stone, six-foot-eight-inch Afro-American named Clay Earl Tave, who was to become one of her most faithful employees.

The real achievement, however, was hers and hers alone. She had written most of the songs, designed the sets, choreographed the dance routines and performed the whole thing. She even did her own make-up. No-one watching the final performance could have guessed that this really was a first for her. She gave a completely professional and assured performance at each venue – the result of extensive rehearsals and unremitting hard work.

7
THE MARRIAGE OF
THE DECADE

Immediately after the tour, Sire decided to release a second single from the *Like A Virgin* album and 'Material Girl' was chosen. A video was needed and the same team who had made the 'Like A Virgin' video – director Mary Lambert and producer Simon Fields from Limelight Productions – were chosen. During the making of the 'Material Girl' video, Madonna was visited on set by someone who had specially requested a meeting with her – Sean Penn, a talented young actor and the brother of Christopher Penn whom Madonna knew from the previous year when he'd used her song 'Burning Up' for his film *The Wild Life*.

For some time, Madonna and Jellybean Benitez had been drifting apart, a rift widened by her absence on tour and all the additional pressures that her stardom was bringing to bear on the relationship. She liked Sean immediately – she was attracted by 'dark brooding men with rough tempers' – and felt that they had a lot in common. For a start, they were surprised to discover that Sean's birthday fell one day after Madonna's. She was 26, he was two years her junior. 'He had a rebellious bad boy image,' she said later, 'the same as I did, only for a girl.'

The other thing that they had in common from the outset was their professionalism and determination to reach the top through sheer hard work. In the previous five years Sean had starred in seven major feature films and in a play on Broadway, and as far as the movie moguls were concerned he was very hot property indeed.

Sean's route to the top of his profession had been more direct than Madonna's, however, since he came from an acting background and had decided back in high school that he wanted to be an actor. His parents were the actress Eileen Ryan and director Leo Penn, and they had always encouraged the cinematic ambitions of their two sons, Sean and Christopher. When Christopher was 16, he was given a Super-8 movie camera for Christmas and the two boys had made their first film together – a sixty-minute piece entitled *Looking For Someone*. As Sean recalled, 'This was our first experience into films. We had to beg people to be in it. We were out all night in Westwood, shooting in parking lots and doing stunts that nobody would ask a stuntman to do. We'd see what we'd shot the week before and then go out that night to shoot more. We found ourselves jumping off twelve-foot high things onto concrete. We had some great action and got hurt all the time . . . couldn't admit it though, because it was high school and we always had a guy working with us that some girl had a crush on and the girl would say "Oh, can I watch?" So that girl made us all rough it. The one thing they couldn't be around for was the acting. That was always private.'

Among Sean's fellow pupils at the Santa Monica High School, south of Los Angeles, were some other would-be actors later to become members of the derogatorily labelled 'Brat Pack'. These included Emilio Estevez, Martin Sheen's son, Tom Cruise, Rob Lowe, Timothy Hutton, Matt Dillon, Andrew McCarthy and River Phoenix. After graduating from high school, Sean served a two-year apprenticeship with the group Repertory Theatre in Los Angeles and then, with mixed feelings about their usefulness, he decided to enrol in acting classes. He settled on a class run by Peggy Feury, a friend of his parents. Her rigorous four-hours-a-day, four-days-a-week sessions honed the young Sean into an accomplished actor and his professional debut occurred on his nineteenth birthday when he obtained a small part in a 'Barnaby Jones' episode on television, followed almost immediately by other parts in the television series 'Concrete Cowboys' and the TV movie *The Killing of Randy Webster*.

Sean then, as his future wife had done, saved up just enough money to go to New York in search of work. He had seen the script of a new play by Kevin Heelan called *Heartland* and liked it; auditions were being held in New York. The play's director, Art Wolff, recalls that Sean 'walked through the door and was physically right'. His first test was disastrous but they persisted and next time it was vastly different. 'Tears were streaming down

my face,' says Wolff, 'tears were streaming down Sean's face . . .
I walked over, put my arm round Sean and we hugged each other.
It was just extraordinary. I've never done that before and never
done that since.' When *Heartland* opened on Broadway for a limited
three-week run, it brought Sean not only invaluable experience but
also excellent press notices. 'He was the best thing in the show,' Art
Wolff added. 'In addition to having that innate, intuitive talent you
can't teach, he has technique, he's really well trained.'

Next, Sean fought off over 2000 other young hopefuls to win
a role in the film *Taps*, directed by Harold Becker, produced by
Stanley Jaffe and starring Timothy Hutton. It was a difficult role
which required special coaching in military horsemanship. Timothy
Hutton enjoyed working with Sean and comments, 'He's really,
really great. A lot of people would label him shy but it's just that
he has a good sense of himself. He doesn't have to carry on and be
an extrovert because he's got really clear vision. It doesn't surprise
me at all how well he's doing.'

The film was released in 1981, by which time Sean was back
living in Los Angeles where he could indulge his passions for surfing,
listening to music and going to the cinema. The attention that his
performance in *Taps* received made things much easier when he
came to audition for his next movie role as the brash, goofy,
pot-headed surfer Jeff Spicoli in Amy Heckerling's film *Fast Times
At Ridgemount High*. The story is about a group of Californian high
school students desperate to lose their virginity. Amy Heckerling
said of Sean, 'He's going to be an incredible artist. He already is.
I kind of know Sean, but I really just know Jeff Spicoli, for he feels
much more comfortable being a character than just being Sean
Penn.'

During the making of *Fast Times* . . . Sean met the girl who was
to become his first fiancée, Pamela Springsteen, sister of Bruce 'The
Boss'. Even with this new interest in his life, he was too much of
a professional in his approach to acting to let it interfere with the
film-making. 'You can't get involved,' he explained, 'it means too
much. It's a permanent record when you make a movie, and it
means too much to do your silly little playing around. I see a lot of
that happen, and it's a shame. I met Pam and saw her afterwards.'

He further explained his attitude to work and his private life as
follows: 'The only thing I'm certain about is the choices I've made

in relation to acting. The other stuff is just part of the experience, you know, as we go along. I don't mean I'm getting married for the experience of marriage, it is just like you have to keep breathing. I met someone whom I always want to be with, she takes care of me. She knows what I'm doing without me having to say anything. There's not much you can do that you don't regret sometimes, but it doesn't matter. As long as you're acting, it doesn't matter.'

Fast Times . . . was released in 1982 and the following year Sean Penn's next film appeared, another complete change of character. In *Bad Boys*, he plays Mick O'Brien, a sullen sixteen-year-old street punk, one of a number of delinquent inmates in a correction centre who get out of hand. The scene in the film of which he is most proud is that where the prison psychiatrist informs him that O'Brien's girlfriend has just been beaten and raped by his Puerto Rican enemy. 'My temptation at that moment,' Sean recalled, 'was to do what every actor in his right mind would have done: go nuts. And I said: "Can't do it. It'd be nice and theatrical, but it's not true."' So for his scene with the psychiatrist, Sean merely pauses and says awkwardly: 'I just wanna cry.'

The critics praised Sean's portrayal of Mick in *Bad Boys*, especially his unwillingness to glamourize the role: David Ansen in *Newsweek* said that 'he rarely raises his voice but commands the screen as he commands the joint, winning your sympathy without even asking for it.' In *The New Yorker*, Pauline Kael compared the impact of his performance with James Dean or the early work of Marlon Brandon. Richard Rosenthal, who directed Sean in *Bad Boys*, declared him to be 'The most talented young actor in films today.' Perhaps one reason for Sean's success in the film was the lengths to which he would go to research the part. He visited many inmates in correctional institutions, and the tattoo he boasts in *Bad Boys* was a genuine one, done specially for the role.

His next film was Louis Malle's *Crackers*, a reworking in 1984 of the (strangely prophetically titled) *Big Deal on Madonna Street* (to give it its English title, the original Italian being *I Soliti Ignoti*) of 1956, a story which tells of a bunch of incompetent crooks who try to run a pawnshop. Sean was starring alongside Donald Sutherland and Jack Warden, with Wallace Shawn and Larry Riley, but Jeffrey Fiskin's script fell flat and the film is not fit to be compared with Malle's 1981 masterpiece *Atlantic City*.

Sean Penn's career as an actor then returned to the stage, in a limited Broadway run of Robert Allan Ackerman's play *Slab Boys*, where he played a working-class Scotsman, John Byrne. Then his next role was back in films, another extraordinary change from the parts he had portrayed before. In Richard Benjamin's *Racing With The Moon*, he played a shy country boy in 1942, one of two Johnny Appleseeds apprehensively awaiting call-up into the US Marine Corps and having to say good-bye to their girlfriends. He co-starred with Elizabeth McGovern and Nicholas Cage.

Also released in 1984, towards the end of that year, was the Orion Pictures presentation of *The Falcon and the Snowman*, directed by John Schlesinger. This film tells of a pair of unsavoury young men, one a drop-out from college and the other a drugs dealer, who decide to sell secrets to the Russians. Timothy Hutton and Sean played the lead roles.

Such, then, was the run-down of Sean's considerable achievements by the time he met Madonna. He was getting rave reviews as a serious actor on the film and theatre pages of the newspapers, although not such a good press in the news and gossip sections which reported his 'boyish' antics and the hard-living, womanizing lifestyle of the Brat Packers. He was being offered plenty of good, solid acting roles and, it seemed, he could have his pick of the women available in Hollywood too. Perhaps he was in danger of letting success go to his head and getting carried away by the power that celebrity brings. What he needed was a cool, level-headed, equally ambitious and independent woman who could keep him out of trouble.

Soon after the release of *The Falcon and the Snowman*, Sean and Pamela announced that they had broken off their engagement. Neither of them have ever disclosed the reasons for this decision. And then came the momentous meeting with Madonna on the set of 'Material Girl'. The two were immediately inseparable. It was a whirlwind romance. Shortly afterwards Sean had to start work on the film *At Close Range*, directed by James Foley. It turned out to be something of a family affair for him as it featured his brother Christopher and his mother Eileen Ryan in the macabre story of a criminal released from jail who comes back to his home town to murder all those who knew about his illegal activities. The criminal was played by Christopher Walken and his son by Sean.

Pat Leonard had recently written a song for a Paramount Pictures film and he asked Madonna to write the lyrics. Paramount, however, decided not to use the resulting song and Madonna suggested that it was perfect for *At Close Range*. She took her demo tape round to James Foley's house, where Sean was staying, and they all agreed immediately that it was perfect. Madonna felt that the song, 'Live To Tell', would be more suitable in the context of the film if it was sung by a man, but the others had no such doubts and Pat Leonard re-recorded the instrumental backing using the same vocal track from the demo. Following the successful release of the film, 'Live To Tell' was issued as a single and in the week of 7 June 1985 it became Madonna's third number one record in the USA. Another hit, 'Crazy For You', which had reached number one in May 1985, had also been a film soundtrack.

After the filming was finished, Madonna and Sean managed to slip away together for a little break in a small town in Tennessee. There is evidence that her feelings for him were developing rapidly. In the past, when an interviewer had asked her what she thought about marriage, she had replied, 'The best thing about being single is that there's always someone else. Besides I wouldn't wish being Mr Madonna on anybody.' But an interview for *Time* magazine which was published on 27 May 1985, showed a definite change of emphasis and indicated the direction her thoughts were taking: 'I think getting married is probably very challenging and I would definitely like to have a child. I've heard wonderful things about it from people I know who are near my age.' One morning, in their Tennessee hotel room, Madonna was 'jumping up and down on the bed, performing one of my morning rituals and all of a sudden he got this look in his eye and I knew what he was thinking. I said "Whatever you're thinking I'll say yes to." That was his chance so he popped it.' There was no question of Madonna not accepting his proposal and they celebrated all day in the 7-Eleven, which was all that the one-horse town had to offer.

The press had not been slow to pick up on Madonna's relationship with Sean Penn. Pictures of the two of them coming out of nightclubs or restaurants were printed almost daily and the same journalists began to dig into her past to see what could be found there. It was perhaps inevitable that the nude photographs taken eight years previously would surface at some stage – and sure enough they did. As Bob Guccione, the publisher of *Penthouse* magazine reported:

'A great number of Madonna nudes had all surfaced at once and we had the first choice. They came from many different sources, from photography teachers and their students, amateurs and professionals.' Most of them were of little artistic or technical merit, and they were not as sexually explicit and arousing as the pictures that generally appear in *Penthouse*. Guccione realized this and offered Madonna a million dollars to pose for new colour nude photographs – an offer which she declined.

Penthouse magazine was not the only publication catering for its particular market: the millionaire Hugh Hefner, founder of the *Playboy* empire, which incorporated a monthly magazine of the same name, had also been approached with nude Madonna photographs, and in fact *Playboy* was the first on the street – in its issue dated 10 July 1985 – with a selection of these pictures. Innocuous though they were, their appearance after such a long time was nevertheless something which Madonna would have infinitely preferred not to have happened, especially when some sections of the press imagined that they had been handed a stick with which to beat her further.

By this time, Madonna had taken a lot of criticism from the press and had developed something of a thick skin about it, but even she was very upset when she learned that *Playboy* magazine had had the 'good taste' to send a set of the pictures to Sean Penn. As she said 'I can't say I wasn't devastated by the experience. When people saw them they thought, "What's the big deal here?" Sean kept saying, "Look, this is all going to blow over." But nobody wants their skeletons to come out of the closet. No matter how successful you want to be, you can never ever anticipate that kind of attention, the grand scale of it all. The thing that annoyed me most was the fact that, for the first time in several years of careful planning and knowing what was going to happen, I felt really out of control. It took me by surprise. It reminded me of the time when I was a little girl at school and the nuns used to come along and lift your dress up in front of everybody to check what colour knickers you were wearing. It's embarrassing because you're just not ready for it and you feel so exposed. Now I look back and I feel silly that I ever got so upset, but I remember feeling that same, end-of-the-world feeling the day my stepmother told me I couldn't wear stockings to school. I cried for hours and thought I wouldn't live through the next day. You think it's the end of the world, and then one day it's not.'

It was a hectic week all round: the *Playboy* pictures hit the streets on 10 July; three days later 'the greatest show on earth' – Live Aid – was beamed from London and Philadelphia throughout the world to an estimated one-and-a-half billion people, almost one in three of the world's total population. Live Aid was the brain-child of Bob Geldof, lead singer of The Boomtown Rats, and came about through the television reports of the devastating famine which was ravaging the peoples of Ethiopia and other parts of the African continent. Building on the massive success of the single 'Do They Know It's Christmas?', Geldof and Midge Ure of Ultravox planned a trans-global link-up of a massive live rock concert, lasting ten hours, with just about every major rock star donating their services. Madonna volunteered to take part in the American concert and appeared on stage at the John F. Kennedy Stadium in Philadelphia on Saturday, 13 July at 4.30 in the afternoon before 90,000 people in the auditorium, and countless millions of television viewers worldwide. It was three days after the *Playboy* nude pictures had been published and by this time, they had been reproduced all over the world. She can't have been too pleased when Bette Midler introduced her to the audience by saying that Madonna was 'A woman who pulled herself up by her bra straps, and has been known to let them down occasionally.'

But Madonna's character, although wounded by the publication of the photographs, was strong enough not to let her be defeated by it. 'Part of me felt about "this" big', she said, 'and another part of me was saying, "I'll be damned if I'm gonna get out there and kick ass, get this dark cloud from over my head."' She demonstrated her determination by retorting to Ms Midler – and to cries of 'Take it off' from the audience – 'I ain't taking nothing off today, they might remember it eight years later'. There were other repercussions after the publication of the photos: the Mayor of Bay City, Michigan, publicly withdrew the offer to Madonna of the Key to the City, saying, 'It would not be in good taste to give it to her now.' But Sean stood by her throughout the whole upsetting affair, giving her his total support and encouraging her just to wait till it all blew over.

As Madonna and Sean celebrated their birthdays on successive days – 16 and 17 August – they decided to make that year's forty-eight hours a triple celebration by marrying on Madonna's 27th birthday, after an engagement of only three months. Because of the publicity which had attended them both during the preceding months, the couple decided to avoid a 'show business' wedding and marry as privately as possible in the grounds of a beautifully appointed cliff-top house in Point Durne, near Malibu Beach, west of Los Angeles, and not far from Santa Monica where Sean was born and brought up. They tried to keep it secret from the press, but one of the invitations got into the hands of a journalist and the story was out. It read: 'Please come to Madonna and Sean Penn's birthday party on 16 August. The celebration will begin at 6pm. Be prompt or you will miss the wedding.' Journalists speculated wildly about the location and hired helicopters to scour the area on the day. Some thought that guests would be airlifted to a wild spot in the middle of California's mountains for an open-air ceremony; others predicted that it would take place in the privacy of her manager's Los Angeles mansion.

The wedding was a small affair by most standards, with only about eighty guests gathered on the lawn by the swimming pool to witness the ceremony. Cher came with her boyfriend Josh Donen; Diane Keaton, Carrie Fisher, Andy Warhol, Martin Sheen and Christopher Walken were among the friends present. Madonna wore a strapless white taffeta and chiffon dress, topped off with a bowler hat and veil.

They were about halfway through the ceremony when the air was shattered by a cluster of helicopters, each one containing a photographer anxious to get a shot of the party. The private nature of the ceremony was completely ruined by the noise and downward draft of the helicopters. Madonna recalled, 'It was almost too much . . . it turned into a circus. In the end, I was laughing. You couldn't have written it in a movie. No-one would have believed it. It was like a Busby Berkeley musical.' Eventually, the intruding air snoopers – forced into such extreme moves by the tight security at the cliff-top house – left, and at last the newly-weds and their guests were left to the celebrations.

About an hour after the ceremony, Sean spotted a partially hidden camera in the clothing of Kip Rano, a British photographer then living in Los Angeles, who had successfully gatecrashed the event. Sean grappled with Mr Rano and they both ended up on the floor before being separated by security men. Mr Rano, speaking afterwards, said 'I blocked his blows and didn't return them because he was obviously drunk. Instead, I grabbed his wrists and we fell to the floor as we struggled. I didn't want to make the situation worse by hitting him; I knew I was on his turf, and I didn't want to rub it in.'

Mr Rano was ejected and the celebrations continued. The music for the reception included several of Madonna's own records, notably 'Into The Groove', but during and after the couple's cutting of their seven-tiered wedding cake, songs by Cole Porter, Bing Crosby, Sarah Vaughan and Ella Fitzgerald regaled the guests.

Shortly before midnight, Madonna and Sean left for their wedding night, which was spent at his parents' home, half a mile away, the newly-weds being driven there in Sean's wedding present for Madonna, a 1956 white and coral convertible Ford Thunderbird. But midnight ushered in Sean's own 25th birthday, and the party continued with more guests at the new venue. Later that day, on the 17th, they left for their secret honeymoon on the idyllic island of Antigua in the British West Indies, sufficiently far from the madding crowd of newshounds to be a safe haven for them.

Once the press have got their teeth into a likely subject, though, they won't give up until they have wrung every last drop of scandal from it. While the couple were on their honeymoon, the press found Camille Barbone, the female partner of Gotham Productions, who had signed Madonna before Sire Records and then failed to hang on to her. Camille obviously still felt bitter about this experience because the tone of her 'revelations' about Madonna's early career is very angry. Among other sordid claims, she told the press that Madonna had seduced and gone to bed with an average of two men a week during the year that she had known her. One wonders how she would have had any time left to work at her music! Of course, it was exactly what the newsmen wanted to hear and Sean and Madonna returned from Antigua to find Camille's stories splashed all over the front pages of the papers.

The problem was that the press – mostly men – could not and still cannot bear to see a successful woman who also has a sex life, who flirts and uses men in the way that men have traditionally used women, and that was what Madonna portrayed in her stage act. They were not going to rest until they had seen their subject and her new husband publicly crucified. A year after her marriage, Madonna said: 'From the time we got married, I got the feeling that people wanted our marriage to fail. They couldn't make up their minds: they wanted me to be pregnant, or they wanted us to get a divorce. That put a lot of strain on our relationship after a while. It's been a character-building experience, and a test of love to get through it all. A lot of times the press would make up the most awful things that we had never done, fights that we never had. Then sometimes we would have a fight, and we'd read about it, and it would be almost spooky, like they'd predicted it or they'd bugged our phones or they were listening in our bedroom. It can be very scary if you let it get to you.

'We are a "Hollywood couple" so people are going to pay a lot of attention to our marriage and whether it's going to work or not. If we have our fights . . . I think that's pretty normal for young people in the first few years of marriage. It's normal for anybody who's married, but when you put all the pressure that we've had on top of that, I think the fact that we're still together is pretty amazing. You know, we're working it out, it's easy to give up but not easy for me to give up.'

At first they lived in an apartment in New York but found that it did not offer enough privacy so they searched around on the West Coast and eventually found a home they both liked in Beverly Hills. The British *News of the World* commented: 'Madonna and Sean Penn's mansion is low key, tasteful and discreet – everything in fact its millionaire owners aren't . . . it'll sure give them something to bicker over in a mega-bucks divorce settlement.' It's little wonder that Madonna has become more and more obsessed with privacy and security, fitting their new home with elaborate security devices and hiring minders to accompany her everywhere she goes.

The adverse press coverage, however, did not discourage her millions of fans all over the world, who wrote expressing their support and encouragement. In the autumn of 1985 Madonna settled down to work on her third album, *True Blue*.

During 1985 sales of her first album had almost topped the three million mark in the USA alone; the *Like A Virgin* album had sold nearly five million copies in America, and nearly three million more world-wide. She had enjoyed three number one USA singles altogether – six weeks at the top position from 22 December 1984 for 'Like A Virgin'; in May 1985 the single 'Crazy for You'; and in June 1985 'Live to Tell'. But in Great Britain her singles success was unprecedented: during 1985 she had had three number one singles out of a total of eight top ten records in the UK chart, the longest succession of such hits ever by a female artist, and the most any artist had achieved in a single calendar year amounting to a total of 84 weeks on the charts. Such extraordinary world-wide public acceptance, together with the support of her new husband, helped Madonna to shrug off whatever apprehension she may have felt regarding the bad publicity being levelled against her. Indeed, her next project could not have been contemplated without an out-going and positive attitude both on Madonna's part and on that of her new husband.

8

SHANGHAI SURPRISE

It was obviously a commercial idea to feature such a famous couple as Madonna and Sean in a film together and a number of companies expressed interest. The British HandMade Films organization, headed by George Harrison, won the day, offering them the lead roles in a new romantic adventure film, to be directed by Jim Goddard. Goddard was a highly respected television director, but this would be his first feature film. Madonna liked the script, and was particularly pleased with the part she was to play in it because it was almost exactly the opposite from that which she had played in *Desperately Seeking Susan*. As she described it, the girl in the proposed film was 'someone very removed from how I actually am, someone who didn't know how to express her emotions. I still needed a role where I could prove to people that I could really act.' Sean 'really liked the male role so we looked at each other and thought "Maybe this would be a good one to do together." We were both setting ourselves up for a challenge, the challenge of being married and working together. A lot of people said it was a sure way to end a relationship. . . .'

But nothing ventured, nothing gained. In January 1986 Madonna and Sean Penn travelled to Shanghai, the setting for the film, *Shanghai Surprise*. The surprise at first was Madonna's. Shanghai is China's largest and most populous city, with around twelve and a half million people, and it is also one of the world's great sea-ports. Madonna and Sean arrived there at about three in the morning. 'But we couldn't sleep,' she recalled, 'so we ended up walking around the streets on this cold morning. It was still dark and the streets were filled with people doing their traditional, slow-motion

Tai Chi exercises. It was so dreamlike. I loved that and because I had blonde hair they thought I was a Martian.' A big plus was that she could move about unrecognized, both of them freed from the prying eyes of the paparazzi, but those idyllic days were shattered when they flew the eight hundred miles south-west to Hong Kong, where the world's press had arrived ahead of them.

The film was set in the old International Settlement part of Shanghai, which formed the basis for the modern commercial heart of the city. It was created in 1863 by the British and United States governments, both of whom had acquired concessions from the Imperial Chinese Government; France also had a concession, but kept separate from the Anglo-US International Settlement, which had its own police force, legal system and courts and armed forces. Because of these difficulties *Shanghai Surprise* could not be filmed in the city itself, and was scheduled to be made on location in Hong Kong. This was fraught with difficulties: in normal circumstances, motion-picture production forms a major source of revenue for Hong Kong, so technically there should have been no problems. Even the extraordinarily cramped social conditions of the island (around five million people in a total area of less than four hundred square miles) ought not to have created difficulties, but location work demands fair weather, a very experienced crew and the minimum of outside interference. But the weather was bad, the director was inexperienced, and the entire crew found themselves on the one hand being followed at every turn by hordes of newspapermen and on the other being obliged to film in the most decrepitly ramshackle and criminally dangerous parts of Hong Kong. This last was no joke: 'protection' was demanded – and paid – daily, but even then rival gangs would sometimes make filming intolerable. As Madonna recalled, 'We were at this one location for eighteen hours because they had blocked the only exit. And this guy wanted fifty thousand dollars to move. That went on every day, and nobody would help us.'

Small wonder then that stories soon began to circulate concerning the filming difficulties. 'We were in a very foreign country working with a Chinese crew and there were communication problems,' Madonna remembers. She 'had to keep walking around in thin cotton blouses in very cold weather, there were big rats underneath our trailers and people were always going down with food poisoning.

I kept saying, "I can't wait till I can look back on all this." It was a survival test – all the odds were against us.'

This was no exaggeration, and matters were made very much worse when they travelled to Macao – a tiny, six-square-mile peninsula west of Hong Kong with a population of a quarter of a million – for more filming. When Madonna and Sean arrived at their hotel, they found a newspaper photographer lurking in their room, hoping to catch an intimate shot of them together. Sean did what many other men would have done in similar circumstances, in twisting the man's camera strap around his neck and throwing him out.

George Harrison himself flew to the stricken crew, but as a musician whose life had become public property at the height of the Beatles' fame, he must have realized that there was little he could do to fend off the newshounds. Several major indoor scenes still had to be shot in England, at Shepperton Film Studios, in Middlesex, and in a disused sanitarium in Virginia Water, in Surrey. On 21 February, Madonna flew to Heathrow, ahead of Sean, to be greeted by an army of newspapermen, reporters and photographers, who besieged her upon her arrival to the extent that when her Mercedes limousine tried to edge itself clear of the pressing throng on leaving the terminal, several reporters were slightly injured, including one from the *Sun*, Britain's biggest-selling daily newspaper, who sprained his foot. The following day's headline, 'Maimed By Madonna', confirmed for her that the press attention in England was not going to be any less than it had been in the Far East, and it was generally almost entirely hostile.

Once again, Madonna and Sean and the rest of the crew had to contend with snoopers on the sets, hidden photographers in hotel rooms, jostling in the street and even theft of pictures from the production company. Once again, George Harrison tried to defuse the situation, and called a press conference at the Kensington Roof Garden on 6 March. This was a very strained occasion, with Madonna exhibiting the patience of a saint in fending off the hawkish and frequently offensively taunting questions. Although she refused to be drawn by them, she soon learned that even her most heartfelt and straightforward response – 'I have nothing to apologize for' – was turned on her in the days that followed. She also learned that in a battle-game with a hostile press, the press owns both the bat and the ball. Despite the old adage that 'It doesn't matter what they say about you, so long as they spell your name right', the facts are that it is nice to have a friend or two on one's side, and at that time Madonna had every reason to think that she did not have even that. In the circumstances, it is little short of amazing that even a passable film was the result of these months of tension and unpleasantness.

It was not entirely unexpected when *Shanghai Surprise*, described as 'a romantic adventure for the dangerous at heart', received a thorough-going critical pasting when it was eventually released in 1986. The story is set in Shanghai in 1937/1938, at the time of the Japanese occupation; a large amount of opium disappears when its owner is murdered trying to escape to the International Settlement. A year later, a missionary base in that settlement has heard of the existence of the opium and engages a 'street-wise tie salesman' (Sean Penn) to track it down, so that it can be used as an anaesthetic for the victims of the current war between China and Japan. Madonna plays Gloria Tatlock, a young virginal American missionary who is entrusted with accompanying the tie salesman, Glendon Wasey. A series of extraordinary adventures befall them before the final denouement and, of course, Madonna and Sean's characters fall in love. The story, with its cross-plots, false trails and double- and triple-crosses, bears a family resemblance to the mistaken identities of *Desperately Seeking Susan*.

The film was based on the novel *Faraday's Flowers* by Tony Kenrick, and the screen-play was written by John Kohn and Robert Bentley. The treatment of the original story is light but the problems that cast and crew encountered during the shooting would have stretched to the utmost the skill and diplomacy of an experienced film-maker, let alone someone such as Jim Goddard who was making his first feature film. All in all, *Shanghai Surprise* remains a difficult memory for most of the protagonists, as Madonna's reflection suggests: 'The film was edited as an adventure movie and they left out all the stuff that was its saving grace. They cut all my major scenes down to nothing which made me look like an airhead girl without any character.' Her final verdict was: 'It was a truly miserable experience that I learned a lot from and don't regret.'

Madonna and Sean returned home to America chastened by their experience in making *Shanghai Surprise* and by their mauling at the hands of the British press. Sean's run-ins with the paparazzi meant he was no stranger to physical mauling, but Madonna – who had to have police protection when she left the Kensington rooftop press conference – must have begun to imagine that she was some kind of femme fatale, bordering on the criminal. 'I thought to myself,' she later said, ' "Am I really this awful? Or does Lucretia Borgia step out in my shoes when I'm not looking?" '

It was not all doom and gloom: there was a pleasant moment in London when Madonna and Sean met Chrissie Hynde and her then husband Jim Kerr. Chrissie, from The Pretenders, had shared what passed for a dressing-room with Madonna backstage at the Live Aid concert, and Jim's band, Simple Minds, was in the British capital on a world tour. The four became very good friends in London, sharing, as they did, the problems of a music-show business marriage. And although Madonna could have been forgiven for overlooking the fact, in view of the press treatment, her British fans had remained loyal – and were remaining so – as her record sales showed. It is interesting to note that although *Shanghai Surprise* bombed when it was released in the cinema and ultimately lost a lot of money, this 'failure' did not seem to detract from Madonna's popular following at all. She continued to be seen as a role model for millions of girls and a sex symbol for the boys, and her record sales with the *True Blue* album, released in summer 1986, went through the roof.

Madonna left England sadder and wiser, but no less determined to make her mark as a serious actress. Back in America there was much to do, much to look forward to, and much to take her mind away from the problems of *Shanghai Surprise*. One of the first matters that demanded her attention was a new film, provisionally entitled *Blind Date*. This seemed promising (the story had nothing in common with two previous films made with the same title), and had the added attraction – as she claimed – that she had the right of approval over the leading man and the director. But, as she said, 'They didn't tell me that they'd already hired Bruce Willis.' For reasons which Madonna has diplomatically failed to reveal, the casting 'just didn't work out'.

Another more important project – entirely hers, over which she could exert complete artistic control – was now coming to fruition, and that was her third album, *True Blue*. 'She was around for every note,' Pat Leonard recalled, and for the first time in her career she was author, or co-writer, of all the songs and credited as co-producer for the entire album. Steve Bray commented upon Madonna's studio work on the *True Blue* album, saying that 'The most interesting thing about being in the studio with Madonna was being on the "Madonna Diet". This consists of not eating at all until we were done with the day's sessions, which often would be 9 p.m. or later. When Madonna got going in the studio, she wanted to keep working until we were finished.'

The single 'Live To Tell', which had made number one in the US in June, had to be included and the follow-up single chosen was 'Papa Don't Preach', a song which would provoke a lot of controversy.

The opening track on the *True Blue* album, 'Papa Don't Preach', has the most startling opening to any Madonna song yet: a powerful symphonic string section, worthy of one of the world's great Philharmonic orchestras, immediately catches the attention. Before the rock instruments enter, it could be the start of a work by Benjamin Britten or Shostakovitch. When Madonna's voice comes in she is singing low in her register in a quiet 'little girl' voice, tinged with sadness and conspiratorially quiet. She is a girl in trouble, telling her father that she's pregnant, she's decided to keep her baby and she doesn't want him to 'preach' at her. This was a subject that would obviously strike a chord with all of her young female fans and the song attracted a storm of protest from the self-appointed moral majority across the United States, who thought it encouraged teenage pregnancy. Alfred Mann, the executive director of Planned Parenthood in New York, said: 'What makes "Papa Don't Preach" so destructive is that she has more impact on teenagers than any other single entertainer. The message is that having a baby is cool, and don't listen to your parents, the school or anybody else who tells you otherwise,' and Dr Sam Jones of the NY medical college went further: 'Madonna is a corrupting Pied Piper, leading impressionable young girls down the primrose path to a depraved and degrading lifestyle.' In fact they have misinterpreted the message and missed the point entirely. The singer regrets what has happened but she is talking to her father about it and asking for his support rather than condemnation. Having a baby is not at all 'cool' in such circumstances, but something disturbing and worrying – hence the tone. The use of the words 'Papa', 'preach' etc. suggest religious connotations

– perhaps Madonna is also talking to the Catholic church here, suggesting that rather than condemning pre-marital sex outright, they should be providing support for children in what is actually a reality of today's society.

Madonna's attitude towards Catholicism at this stage of her life is somewhat contradictory. Was the use of rosaries and crucifixes as costume jewellery tongue-in-cheek or something deeply felt? The old adage 'once a Catholic, always a Catholic' has a lot of truth in it and after such a strict upbringing in the faith as Madonna had received, it would be quite astonishing to find that she'd broken away from it entirely. In fact, she described her feelings in an interview in 1985 as follows: 'Catholicism gives you an inner strength whether you end up believing it later or not. I don't go to church but I believe in God. I think I have always carried around a few rosaries with me. There was the turquoise-coloured one that my grandmother had given to me a long time ago. One day I decided to wear it as a necklace. It isn't a sacrilegious thing for me.'

So the song 'Papa Don't Preach' was not an incitement to rebellion on the part of her followers, but rather Madonna addressing herself to a serious, universal problem and asking parents (and the church) to show understanding rather than straightforward condemnation based on antiquated moral standards.

'Open your Heart', the next song on *True Blue*, is another very powerful song with a body-popping medium funk rhythm and an unpredictable scrap of a tune. Madonna is again singing at the lowest end of her range, and her voice is embroidered by the elegant chiming of antique Chinese cymbals. The message of the hook line, 'Open your heart to me, baby/I hold the lock and you hold the key', is full of classic Madonna double entendres. She is pleading with a seemingly indifferent boy to be open with her so that she can feel secure and loved, but flirting with him at the same time suggesting that his 'key' would fit into her 'lock'. The video made for this song was another controversial one as she portrayed a seductive peep-show artist being observed by a young boy (played by Felix Howard).

The third song, 'White Heat' is introduced by a scrap of dialogue from the 1949 James Cagney film, just at the point when he realizes his fellow prisoner, Edmund O'Brien, is a government agent. The part Cagney played, of a violent repressed homosexual with a profound Oedipus complex, was sensational at the time and the film is, for many, one of the great all-time gangster movies. Madonna's song, however, dedicated to Jimmy Cagney, is not one of her best. Co-written with Pat Leonard, it's an experimental number with a deep funk bass line and an adventurous instrumental break; Madonna's voice is strong but the lyrics are innocuous and the whole doesn't quite come off. The fourth song and the last on side one is 'Live to Tell', which was originally written for the Sean Penn film, *At Close Range*.

The second side of the album begins with a tremendous dash of colour, a complete change of pace and style with 'Where's The Party?', written by Madonna with Steve Bray and Pat Leonard. It is a sort of funky-rock song, resting heavily on a bass-line of immense energy and syncopation with sudden flashes of lightning-tunes cutting through the air. She sings of working Monday through Friday keen for the weekend to come so that she can party.

The album's title track, 'True Blue', opens another door for us: a soft reminiscence of late 1950's rock'n roll with gently throbbing triplets and a small string section in Buddy Holly/Everly Brothers style. Then, 'La Isla Bonita' is as stylish a recreation of samba-bossa nova music as 'True Blue' was of its period. A catchy medium-tempo calypso beat ushers in the song, softly-struck percussion riding across a friendly Caribbean bass and beneath the Madonna fingerprint: adjacent chords. Even the sound of her voice is in the proper al fresco style as she sings 'Last night I dreamt of San Pedro/just like I'd never gone, I knew the song/A young girl with eyes like the desert.' This is another collaborative effort, between Madonna, Pat Leonard and Bruce Gaitsch, with Gaitsch himself playing outstanding Hispanic acoustic guitar.

If the two previous songs were inspired by nostalgic popular music styles, with 'Jimmy, Jimmy' we are plunged back into slightly more recent urban rock, a faster bouncy number in which the girl – in love with Jimmy, who is something of a waster and squanderer – sings to him, begging him to change his ways and bemoaning their likely fate. 'Why do fools fall in love with fools like you?' The concluding song is 'Love Makes the World Go Round', another Madonna-Pat Leonard collaboration. A different musical influence – that of reggae – bursts this song into life with a street carnival tapestry of extreme tightness and florid energy. But it is the experience of Band Aid that is perhaps the greater influence, as Madonna sings 'There's hunger everywhere/We've got to take a stand/Reach out for someone's hand/Love makes the world go round' – which is a clear reference to the universal attempts to alleviate third world famine. And yet, whilst it would have been too easy to have written some kind of aching blues number, bemoaning the global situation and bewailing the fate of our fellow-men, Madonna's response is immensely up-lifting in a positively vibrant manner. 'Love Makes The World Go Round' is a tremendous reggae-style track, brilliant in its realization and a good dance number.

As with her previous two albums, Madonna dedicated the *True Blue* collection, this time 'To my husband, the coolest guy in the universe'. Taken overall, her third album is a remarkable achievement. Whilst it has its less-than-compelling moments, the level of invention is astonishingly high, and the album's consistency is perhaps its most lasting factor. It continued the phenomenal run of chart success Madonna had enjoyed by providing a whole series of top ten single hits. 'Papa Don't Preach' followed 'Live to Tell' as a number one hit in America; in the UK 'Live to Tell' reached number two and 'True Blue' became number one in October 1986, staying in the charts for three months. This confounded the British press antagonists of earlier in the year, for the UK success surpassed her current American chart placings. 'True Blue' was a US top ten hit, but it got no higher than three. In America, however, 'Open Your Heart', released as the fourth single from the *True Blue* album, made the USA number one spot in February of 1987. Although Madonna is credited as co-writer with Gardner Cole and Peter Rafelson, the two gentlemen originally wrote it as 'Follow Your Heart', a rock-and-roll number for Cyndi Lauper (who, coincidentally, had a parallel American hit in February 1987 with a similarly titled song, 'Change of Heart'). When it was offered to Madonna for her consideration, she surprised everyone by selecting it and changing certain aspects to fit the kind of musical direction into which she wanted to move. She altered the words here and there, and she and Pat Leonard, as Bennett Freed – Gardner Cole's manager – explained, added a 'bass line underneath the song and got it into a rock and roll dance area instead of just rock and roll. The original song was more pop/rock than dance. Pat and her just cut it into a dance song.' It turned out to be the first song Madonna recorded for the album, and may have set the general tone for *True Blue* itself.

The British success of 'Open Your Heart' – it got to number four in December of 1986 – completed a colossal two years of unprecedented chart domination by Madonna. If one counts the original releases of 'Holiday', 'Lucky Star' (number 14 in March 1984, and on the charts for nine weeks), and 'Borderline' (relatively unsuccessful when first issued in May 1984, peaking at number 56), this makes almost exactly three years of best-selling singles, with no failures in between. In 1985 Madonna dominated the British singles charts with 84 weeks of placings; Bruce Springsteen was second with 45 weeks. In 1986 she again dominated the same charts with 59 weeks of placings, becoming the first person since Elvis Presley in 1971 to retain the top position for two years running.

The gold mine that the *True Blue* album had become had not yet run out: 'La Isla Bonita' – originally intended by Pat Leonard for Michael Jackson, but turned down by him – was Madonna's next single, becoming the fifth consecutive top five single from the album in the USA in May 1987, but in the UK it went straight into the charts at number 5, then to number 2 and finally number 1, when it supplanted the British Ferry Aid single (another charity record, issued to help the dependents of those lost in the North Sea 'Herald of Free Enterprise' ferry disaster, when almost two hundred people died as the vessel capsized on leaving Zeebrugge harbour).

The album *True Blue* achieved a deserved, but nonetheless phenomenal, success with worldwide sales approaching twelve million. It also became a number one best-selling album in twenty-eight countries – a feat described by the 1989 edition of the *Guinness Book of Records* as being 'a totally unprecedented achievement' – certainly a feat which has not seemed like being approached, let alone surpassed, since.

Perhaps her chart success had given her a calmer self-confidence, helped – at least at first – by her marriage, as well as financial security for life, if she wanted it. Towards the end of 1986 and in the early months of 1987, Madonna seemed to have become more settled as a person. Pat Leonard noted this, and commented 'I've seen her change a lot in the last two years. When it first all turned up, she kept fighting to make sure it didn't go away. Now there's a lot more trusting. She doesn't think it's going to go away.' Nor should it, for such was her creativity that others were coming to her for help. As producer of her own multi-million selling album, she was now effectively mistress in her own studio. Warner Brothers asked her to write a song for Nick Kamen (up to then best known as the young man who stripped to his underpants in the laundrette to the strains of 'Heard It Through The Grapevine'). She came up with 'Each Time You Break My Heart', which she not only wrote herself but also produced, and it reached number one in Britain, knocking the last Wham! single from the top position. It was the first time a single written and produced by a woman for a man had achieved this accolade; what was even more unusual was that Madonna did not appear on it. As if to acknowledge the loyalty of her British fans, Madonna agreed to undertake concerts in the UK in 1987 as part of a projected world tour, and gave an interview for the BBC's Radio 1 at the turn of the year.

Her new-found, more relaxed and philosophical self-confidence had also healed any remaining breaches that might have existed with her family. Reunited at Thanksgiving 1986, the Ciccone children (now all adult) had group photographs taken. Each pursuing individual careers at that time, it was exceptional for them all to be in the one place at the same time. Madonna said afterwards that she felt that at last, now she was an established artist, her father had given his approval. 'I think my father really understands what I was trying to do. Nowadays he's very happy and proud of me.'

9

WHO'S THAT GIRL?

The director of *At Close Range*, James Foley, had also directed Madonna's videos for 'Live to Tell' and 'Papa Don't Preach'; no more different subject could have been chosen by him for his next film, *Who's That Girl?*, the screenplay of which he had shown to Madonna in July 1986. As Madonna recalled, Foley 'knew that I'd wanted to do a comedy for a long time, so it was like my reward. There was just something about the character, the contrasts in her nature, how she was tough on one side and vulnerable on the other, that I thought I could take and make my own. I just love those films where the woman gets away with murder, but her weapon is laughter, and you end up falling in love with her.'

In many senses, *Who's That Girl?* was as complete a change of part for Madonna from Gloria Tatlock in *Shanghai Surprise* as Brad Junior in *At Close Range* had been for Sean from Glendon Wasey. Superficially, it might seem to have marked for Madonna a return to *Desperately Seeking Susan*, for the locale – New York – is the same, and she is pretty much as streetwise here as Susan was, except that the character she plays in *Who's That Girl?*, Nicole (Nikki) Finn, is much more primitively innocent and far less practical. She compared the role to the kind of Judy Holliday dumb blonde part in which she 'could really come off as being dumb, but she knew exactly what was going on'. Perhaps a telling remark she made in the wake of the commercial failure of *Shanghai Surprise* – 'It's deadly when you try and second-guess public opinion. Your best bet is to stay true to yourself' – indicates how hurt she must have been by the whole episode. Nevertheless, as Nikki, Madonna was given a great chance to shine in a classic screwball comedy, and she grasped this opportunity with considerable élan. In addition, this film was one in which for the first time she was undoubtedly the star.

The plot of *Who's That Girl?* tells the bizarre story of about thirty-six hours in the life of Nikki Finn, after she has been released from prison on parole for a murder she strenuously denies having committed. Loudon Trott (played by Griffin Dunne) has been sent by his boss to ensure that she gets straight on a bus to Philadelphia but she is determined to try and clear her name and the two get caught up in a string of adventures involving a rare cougar, which Trott has agreed to pick up for a client. They are also being tailed by a pair of detectives – cue some car chase scenes – and the final denouement takes place when Madonna interrupts a wedding ceremony to announce that she has uncovered the real murderer.

In addition to starring in this film, Madonna wrote and sang four new songs based on the characters and situations in the film. These are: 'The Look of Love', 'Causing a Commotion', 'Can't Stop' and 'Who's That Girl?'.

The making of *Who's That Girl?* posed a number of problems, but those which might have attended Madonna's part as Nikki were swiftly disposed of by the actress. 'I think we're always attracted to characters when there's something of ourselves there. I had a lot in common with Nikki. She's courageous and sweet and funny and misjudged. But she clears her name in the end, and that's always good to do. I'm continuously doing that with the public. I liked Nikki's tough side and her sweet side. The toughness is only a mask for the vulnerability she feels.'

Her closeness to the part was also echoed by James Foley, who recalled: 'After leaving prison, the world looks wonderful to Nikki. She's incredibly optimistic, which parallels Madonna's natural enthusiasm. She's genuinely happy to be alive.' Foley was also faithful to the story's 'undeniable good humour that seems to carry it effortlessly from the first frame to the last. Even though guns are being fired and cars are whipping around corners, nobody gets hurt and the crimes are all victimless. The most destructive thing that is actually shown on film is what happens to the Rolls-Royce: it just gets stolen, stripped, covered with graffiti, and finally just falls apart from fatigue.'

James Foley also recalled being continuously surprised by

Madonna, who, he said, 'notices the smallest details, and she's always curious. I saw her do things – interpretations, reactions, capture certain moments with a nuance of character twist – that I hadn't thought of. She has an absolute lack of convention in approaching something, and her willingness to try anything, no matter how bizarre, was wonderful.' When Griffin Dunne was chosen as the male lead, Foley recalled that when he 'came in, sat down and read a scene with Madonna, everyone in the room laughed. He was able to reach a level of humour that surpassed our high expectations. Madonna's such a fireball you want a guy to be a comic partner and not just the straight man. During the chaos, his character has to retain his masculinity and his dignity. Griffin did that.'

If the leading roles had been as well filled as those of the sup- porting characters, the most difficult part to cast – the Company has admitted – was that of Murray, the cougar. It was quite clear that a real, live animal had to appear – and at times, on the streets of New York City, for during one scene the animal was required to jump out of a second-storey window, disarm a crook of his knife, and escape with Madonna by running down a street. The production company engaged Hollywood Animals Inc, a specialist firm run by Boone Narr and Sled Reynolds, whose concern at first was how the cast and crew would interact with the cougars. The film's co-producer Bernard Williams said, 'What we constantly had to remember was that whilst the animals may look like big, cuddly cats, they're not.' Boone Narr recalled that 'Madonna was incredible. She immediately understood how to work with these cats.'

She also understood how to charm the crew: Foley remembers, 'They'd run around getting her boxes to sit on, and when it got cold [shooting began in September, and the weather became a problem because the film had to appear as though it was springtime] they'd build her a little booth with a heater and she'd sit in there like a princess and love it. She's the greatest flirt of all time.' Another problem regarding the location was that filming in New York's busy streets was not so straightforward as it had been in the old days; however, the company received the co-operation they needed and were allowed to film at such key locations as the New York Public Library, Trump Tower and Fifth Avenue.

But *Who's That Girl?*, for all the excellence of the various components which went to make it, is essentially Madonna's film, and in three main areas throughout her performance is astonishingly consistent. In the first place, her accent is so idiomatic that at times it is difficult for a non-New Yorker to make out what she is saying. Only in one romantic scene does her voice become subtly less frenetic, emphasizing Nikki's feminine wiles.

The second main area is the visual presentation of the character of Nikki. Her clothing, hairstyle and make-up are quite distinctive, and were recognized as being of supreme importance before the film began to be shot. The costumier for *Who's That Girl?*, Deborah Scott, has spoken of the motives behind her dressing of Madonna as Nikki: 'When I do a movie, I don't usually have to think about what people are going to be wearing in six months, but in this case I did take that into account because there are teenagers all over the world who follow her style. You don't make decisions on that basis, but it definitely has an influence. The clothing then must define a specific character in a certain place and time. It's exciting when the work of a costume designer branches out to influence fashion, but when movies have affected what people wear it has been a matter of chance and timing. The degree of a film's popularity can help create a phenomenon.' Such an approach can only succeed when the star in question agrees with and co-operates fully with the designer. Scott has said that Madonna and Foley were 'wonderful collaborators; we spent a lot of time talking about style ideas, character and the physical demands of the script. I felt lucky to be working with Madonna, who can carry off a variety of different looks. Her appearance changes significantly during the film.'

The third main area where Madonna dominated the film was in her songs. If 'light and airy' describes Madonna's performance in the film as Nikki, such a phrase can also be aptly applied to the title song by Madonna and Pat Leonard, which immediately recalls summertime in the city. The first verse, when it comes, is a delightful mixture of English and Spanish/Puerto Rican, a generous compliment to the New York of mid 1980s, where every official sign and hamburger-bar menu is in both languages. Steve Bray is credited as composer of the film's music, and he collaborated with Madonna on 'Causing A Commotion', which follows the title track on the soundtrack album. Madonna's harmony and cross-phrasing in this are delightful as the rhythmic pulse itself becomes seemingly tighter and tighter throughout the song – matching the lyric ('I've got the move baby, you got the motion. If we got together we'd be causing a commotion'). 'The Look Of Love', the second song by Madonna and Patrick Leonard, is another superbly atmospheric number. Like a half-remembered folk song, it is not at all sophisticated in the metropolitan sense but sedately mild, totally and placidly the expression of a cool yet regretful temperament, at ease, the song flows upon its seemingly effortless and limitless way. The singer, recollecting her lover's departure in tranquillity, is not bitter – just regretful. After this outstanding number, 'Can't Stop' is the final song by Madonna (co-written with Steve Bray) on the album. This is very similar in construction to 'Causing A Commotion', as well as to earlier work by the pair, such as 'Into the Groove' and 'Spotlight'. Rhythmically, the song moves with considerable verve, but in spite of this admirable energy the accent on the second beat of every other bar is not a very subtle touch. The main tune of the song itself is a little too formula-ridden for comfort. Whilst it is not a particularly outstanding example of the work of these writers, there are some nice touches in the song and in the atmosphere created by the production, so that it is not without redemption. Eventually, however, one begins to wonder what Nile Rodgers might have made of this track: probably the funkier aspects would have been heavily emphasized, doubtless to the track's overall improvement.

The *Who's That Girl?* soundtrack album also has songs from Duncan Fauré, Club Nouveau, Michael Davidson, Scritti Politti and Coati Mundi. Altogether the album makes an excellent memento of an enjoyable film, which sadly was poorly received at first, although it did excellent business in Europe. The professional film critics' reactions to *Who's That Girl?* were somewhat mixed and overall uncomplimentary. Madonna must surely have felt that she had given a good performance, but once again, and for the second time in a row, she had failed to strike home in an acting role. There can be little doubt that such an experience made her all the more determined to show what she could do.

In spite of Madonna's continued chart success, there were other disappointments with which to contend. The most serious and personal was the death of Martin Burgoyne. Martin had designed the sleeves for Madonna's first two US twelve-inch singles ('Everybody'

99

and 'Burning Up'/'Physical Attraction'); he had been one of the dancers in Madonna's showcase performance of 'Everybody' and also when she appeared on 'The Tube' in England. He had designed an earlier book on Madonna entitled *Lucky Star* (later re-issued as *Madonna – Her Story*). And he had also offered her shelter on her return from Paris, offering her a hand of friendship at the time when she needed it most. During the previous year he had contracted Aids and Madonna recalls, 'I cried like a baby when Martin told me . . . I still cry when I think about it.' She immediately arranged to pay for his hospitalization and medical expenses, but to no avail. She paid a heavier price than most, in fact, for Sean was angry at first when he found out about her charity. Many people overheard his anger one day on a film lot in Los Angeles: 'You're more concerned about your damned friends than you are about me. You spend more time worrying about friends with Aids.'

'Stop acting like a child,' Madonna is reported to have shouted back. 'Why don't you just run off and get your act together?'

Later on, having recovered something of her composure, she confided that 'For two months Sean and I have been fighting about Martin and the whole Aids thing. But Martin was there for me when I needed him and I feel I should stick by him in his hour of need. I've told him not to worry about medical bills. They will all be paid.'

Sean demanded that she take an Aids test which she refused, claiming that as she and Martin had never had sex the subject was irrelevant. Sean's stand could have done little to repair the fractures that were seen to be appearing in their marriage, which had surfaced towards the end of her filming *Who's That Girl?*, when she spent her spare time slipping away to visit Martin in hospital. During the filming, Sean had stayed at their Malibu home in Los Angeles; their separation fuelled the stories that some folk delight in, but actually he was planning a new movie, set in Los Angeles.

Within a few months of the start of 1987, Martin was dead, in his mid-20s. At around this time, a number of stars – singers, actors and actresses – had decided to do something to raise the public awareness of Aids, as well as some much-needed money for Aids clinics, and to emphasize the fact that it was no longer a disease affecting homosexuals exclusively. Having seen the effects at close hand, Madonna was determined to do something practical to help when her commitments allowed. She modelled a denim jacket designed by Martin at an Aids Charity Research function in Barney's, which was later auctioned with all proceeds going to a supportive care programme for Aids patients at St Vincent's Hospital in New York.

Around this time, Madonna also took up golf and partnered Bob Hope in a charity golf tournament. This was a welcome break for her but Sean, a little frustrated at being constantly separated from his wife and beginning to shoot the new movie, *Colors*, sometimes found his short fuse tending to explode. As he said later, 'When I married Madonna, I certainly didn't expect the kind of ruckus that occurred in the media. I was realistic enough to know it would be louder than quieter, but now I have to be realistic about the elements of my image. I have to pay a little more attention and get you to think about the character I'm playing instead of me.' Earlier, he had said: 'Sean Penn as the husband of a big rock star creates a lot of adrenalin in some people, who will go into a movie with an incredible amount of preconceptions on who I am.'

Madonna was also aware of the tensions with which Sean had to contend: 'He's a very serious actor and he isn't interested in having a Hollywood star image, so it [the publicity surrounding and following their marriage] took him by surprise. We deal with it differently. I don't like violence, I never condone hitting anyone. But on the other hand, I understood Sean's anger and, believe me, I've wanted to hit them many times, but I realize it only makes things worse . . . the press went out of their way to pick on Sean, to the point where they would walk down the street and kind of poke at him and say, "C'mon, hit me."' Nor was this all Sean had to contend with: whilst out walking with Madonna, she recalled, 'They would call me obscene names in front of him just to get him to react, but Sean is trying not to take the bait. He'd have to become a pacifist or a Buddhist to tolerate the baiting he gets.'

It would clearly have taken the patience of a saint for any man to have ignored such intense and deliberate provocation, especially when off-duty, so to speak. He reacted with a couple of punches when a particularly offensive journalist taunted him and Madonna one evening in Los Angeles; of course, a cameraman was in tow to record the event, and Sean was arraigned before a Los Angeles court for assault. He was placed on probation.

The film *Colors* is a serious and violent film about a serious and violent subject – the street gangs of Los Angeles. In it, Sean plays a rookie cop, a little short on subtlety, starring opposite Robert Duval. For whatever reason – perhaps the enforced separation between them on either side of the American continent; or because of the rumours of Madonna's flirtations which had begun to filter through to him; or because of the demands of the part he was playing and the tough neighbourhood in which it was being shot; or because of the offensive nature of the approach of a particularly probing newspaperman, Sean lost his temper again on the set, and floored the reporter and an extra who had attempted to separate them.

This was serious: clearly in breach of the terms of his earlier probation, Sean now faced a sixty-day jail sentence when the case came to court. It was doubly so for Madonna: her husband was likely to go to jail, and she was about to embark upon her most extensive and important tour yet, a world tour which began in Japan in June, during which – with Sean's filming expected to have been finished – she imagined her husband would accompany her. Now, thanks to his temper, he would not. It was trebly so, for publicly she had to perform some kind of balancing act between on the one hand the promotion of her film and the attendant songs, and the natural questions which she would be asked concerning Sean. Whilst on the 'Johnny Carson Show' in May, her first television chat show appearance, she defended Sean: 'He isn't as people imagine him to be. He's quite a shy person by nature. Am I shy? I have to admit that I do flirt a lot, flirting's part of my make-up. I'll flirt with anybody from garbagemen to grandmothers.'

The forthcoming tour had to take precedence: she was to be seen live by over two million people and thanks to the immense amount of preparatory work done by her management and her record company, it turned out to be a sensational triumph. It began in Tokyo at the Korakuen Stadium, where she was scheduled to give three concerts. Her reception at the airport set the standard for the rest of the world tour; not since the Beatles had such a commotion been caused by a pop star. On the opening night, a freak thunderstorm of typhoon proportions blew up which brought the show to a standstill, but the 35,000 and more fans who had sold out the concert for weeks previously would not leave, and began chanting for the typhoon to blow itself out. It did not and the fans eventually dispersed, hours later, drenched to the skin, whilst Madonna, together with the close members of her entourage, repaired to an Italian restaurant in downtown Tokyo. During the meal, a Japanese girl fan of hers endeavoured to get inside the restaurant and approach the star. The girl had obviously been at the stadium: she was soaked, but clutched some souvenir programmes and hesitantly asked Madonna for an autograph.

Many stars would have reacted differently but Madonna, seeing the young girl's plight and evident admiration for her, called her to her table and began signing her programmes. It proved too much for the girl, who burst into tears, and by doing so, affected several people at Madonna's dinner party. As she herself said of the incident, 'When people make themselves that vulnerable, they always endear themselves to me. And yet there was something so servile about it, sometimes it makes you feel like you're enslaving somebody. And that's a creepy feeling.' Perhaps it is, but it is one that Madonna has on more than one occasion been forced to recognize. For she herself, having come such a long way in such comparatively few years, recognized the vulnerable girl, the shy yet adoring fan, was in reality a human being, and meeting Madonna would have been one of the highlights of the young girl's life. Curiously, there was more than an echo of the event in Madonna's stage show, as she fell to the floor whilst a photograph of her gradually faded. As Debbie Voller has described it, 'a gesture of hopelessness – then [she] sprang back up again in defiance – the girl in the gutter, always fighting back and aiming for the stars.' The Japanese girl did not quite fit every aspect of this scene, but the defenceless human being does.

The remaining concerts went off without a hitch, and were sensational in their impact: *Rolling Stone* magazine, hardly the kind of organ one would first think of for a sympathetic appraisal of Madonna's performance, described her appearance thus: 'There has probably never been a more imaginative or forceful showcase for the feminine sensibility in pop than Madonna's current concert tour. She is simply the first female entertainer who has ever starred in a show of this scope, a fusion of Broadway-style choreography and post-disco song and dance that tops the standards set by previous live concert firebrands like Prince and Michael Jackson.' Heady words, indeed, and the more so from such a source: Madonna could hardly have hoped for a better beginning to the tour, but it was soured by the news – as she arrived back in Los Angeles from the long trans-Pacific flight – that Sean had been given a sentence of sixty days in jail for the fracas on the *Colors* set and for reckless driving. The details of the latter charge remain somewhat obscure, even to Madonna: 'At the time I didn't know all the details, and I didn't want to.'

As if publicly to atone for his earlier haranguing of Madonna for her support of Martin Burgoyne during the final months of his life, Sean broke a condition of his bail – granted to enable him to complete his filming – by flying to New York to attend Madonna's appearance at the special Aids Benefit Concert she gave as a tribute to her late friend. Madonna dedicated her performance of 'Live To Tell' to Martin's memory. The Concert raised in excess of $250,000 dollars, and Sean risked imminent arrest by appearing with Madonna on stage whilst she spoke: 'I'm trying to think of something eloquent to say, but I don't want this to be a morbid event. Hopefully, your presence and our help together will help us find a cure for this thing forever.'

Sean's presence in New York, in full view of a large audience, when he should have been completing his film, was in clear breach of the court's dispensation: a warrant was issued for his arrest.

10
THE 1987 WORLD TOUR

With the troubled situation concerning Sean's imminent jail sentence and the enormous pressure upon her as she made the final arrangements for the most important tour of her life, Madonna arrived at New York's JFK Airport to board British Airways' Concorde flight BA2 for London, booked on the flight in her maiden name. The journey began none too well. There were reports of a last-minute acrimonious exchange between Madonna and Sean, and even a preposterous suggestion that Sean had been booked on the plane to travel to London with her (preposterous, for an American citizen, on bail or on probation, or – as with Sean – awaiting a jail sentence to be confirmed, has to surrender his or her passport). More directly troubling was the fact that the flight was delayed for one hour, forty-five minutes before it left New York. These were not good omens.

In fact, because this was Sean's first jail sentence, he would not be treated too harshly: although sentenced to sixty days, this period could be reduced to thirty-two days for good behaviour. He was taken to Bridgeport's Redondo jail in northern California, which contained a special detention centre for first-time short-sentence offenders. How Sean would serve the sentence he had received caused some raised eyebrows: he would do it in parts – six days at first, followed by time away from jail working on location to finish the movie *Colors* (a film about a young tearaway cop) and a return to Bridgeport to complete the sentence. Whilst many felt that the manner of serving the sentence he received was too soft, it was wholly in keeping with the system of jurisprudence then in operation in California.

Madonna was naturally nervous when she boarded Concorde for

London, not least because she was about to appear live for the first time in Britain – her 1983 concerts had been mimed to pre-recorded tapes. A lot of money was at stake, for the concerts were expected to turn over in excess of four million pounds. Under the terms of the new 'withholding tax' in Britain, which had come into effect on 1 May 1987, following the establishment of the principle in the Finance Act of the previous year, the responsibility for deducting the tax, set at a rate of 27 per cent, fell to the promoters, in this case the experienced and highly regarded Harvey Goldsmith organization. However, although the tax payable – in theory – would have amounted to over a million pounds, overheads and other costs had to be deducted, which probably left around 20 per cent profit to which the tax could then be applied. The tax, introduced by Chancellor Nigel Lawson, was an oblique compliment to the enormous power and influence the British music industry had on international stars: in normal circumstances, the prospect of paying such a hefty tax bill at source would have deterred many entertainers from coming to Britain. But as a representative of Harvey Goldsmith's organization is reported to have said: 'Britain is too important a territory for people not to come. It is a big market and important to American stars from a prestige point of view.'

As if to compensate for the new tax, the media coverage accorded to Madonna's British concerts was priceless: during her stay, there could have been very few inhabitants of the British Isles who were not aware of her presence. A lot was at stake concerning this British part of the tour and it rested on her shoulders entirely. No wonder, therefore, that with all this pressure, Madonna refused a supposedly specially prepared meal on the flight and declined to give autographs to airline staff. A few hours on Concorde is not a particularly restful journey but she must have craved a few moments of relaxation. She and her close party were astounded at the reception awaiting at Heathrow. So, for that matter, were the police and airport security staff, as well as Clay Earl Tave, her minder, who had accompanied her on the flight.

Terminal Four at Heathrow Airport is the newest and smallest of the arrival buildings of the world's busiest air terminus. Concorde flights were handled there, together with a few short-hop journeys to Europe and the Mediterranean on conventional aircraft, but no arrival on the supersonic plane had ever before matched the tumult which greeted Madonna on the evening of 13 August 1987. Around a thousand fans, waiting reasonably patiently for the delayed flight, clashed with minders and security staff as Madonna – kept waiting in the customs hall for ten minutes whilst her entire personal baggage was searched – was escorted through the doors into the arrival hall.

She looked superb – at least, to those who managed to catch a glimpse of her through the surging melée – and it was soon obvious that the nine bodyguards employed to look after her would not be sufficient protection against the swamping, jostling crowd. More than thirty uniformed policemen, on standby for just such a situation, crowded round her and formed a wedge-shaped phalanx to force their way out of the exit doors to the waiting limousine. But when they reached the exit doors, they were met by more than one hundred Madonna fans trying to force their way in. Other bona fide passengers were crushed in the scrimmage, including children, and Madonna herself was later reported to have been terrified at what she saw.

It was not over yet. No sooner had she and her minders reached the limousine than they found that an airport bus had pulled up in front of the car, preventing it from leaving quickly. When Madonna's limousine eventually managed to navigate the traffic, more fans lay in its path, blocking its progress, and with others running alongside the vehicle, in the road, endangering themselves in the process, the situation became alarming. But eventually, the limousine and its attendant escort vehicles made the M4 motorway and sped towards London. At the May Fair Hotel in London's West End, Madonna was hurriedly taken to her suite, from where she at last had the peace and safety to reflect on her circumstances. Madonna had arrived.

The next morning, fourteen hours after her reception, Madonna was out early, jogging in Green Park – across the other side of Piccadilly – with bodyguard Clay Tave and a group of minders, along with an armada of paparazzi. Still keeping fit, the more so with the first of the four dates a day or so away, Madonna permitted nothing to interfere with her seven-mile work-out, five circuits of the inner perimeter of the park. Apart from the fitness thing, the running actually helped her to unwind mentally from the pressures of the previous evening. On her return to the May Fair Hotel, she ran the gauntlet of another large group of fans en route and Clay Tave got involved in a scuffle with a photographer, Zahid Hussein. Madonna later ventured out shopping to South Molton Street, which is not too far away but it proved to be another outside trip which was spoiled by having to dodge many followers, almost literally being rescued from the crowds at one point. Maybe she was ill-advised to try it, but she doubtless felt she had every right to shop if she so wished.

The following day she travelled north to Leeds for the first date of the tour. She was driven along the M1 to Luton airport, where she caught a plane for Leeds-Bradford airport. After the scenes at Heathrow, the Yorkshire constabulary were taking no chances: Madonna was whisked safely and speedily to Roundhay Park, just outside Leeds, where she was to rehearse and make the final preparations for that night's concert.

Madonna's opening show was astounding. The press coverage of her visit had been enormous, generating in the process the inevitable reaction: there had been a growing number of commentators who would have relished a perceptible lowering of the expected temperature and would have loved to slam her had the show been less than spectacular. But even the most jaundiced observer would have been left gaping-mouthed at this performance. It began at 8.30 p.m., the day having been cool and somewhat overcast. The crowd was in excess of 70,000 people who had paid an average of sixteen pounds per head (grossing over one million pounds) – an amazing figure considering the location. They became so immediately bound up in the event that an hour later security guards were dousing parts of the audience with water, both to keep them cool and to bar them from getting too close to the stage.

The achievement, secured in July, of becoming the first female singer to have had five number one hit records in the British singles charts, ensured that very many people were familiar with her music. Those who had come expecting the female equivalent of a rock show were confounded: this show had little to do with ethnic rock music, as the opening set lights revealed. An estimated 375 tonnes of equipment had been assembled over the previous three days and the front of the stage had been made to look like the facade of a white theatre, whilst over, above and behind this emphasis on the theatrical the main area of the stage was constructed like some early 1930s Busby Berkeley/Sol Polito set extravaganza – but in colour.

There were flights of steps and stairways, beautifully set off with richly hanging curtains. Taking several leaves from the late Sean Kenny's originality of stage movement, parts of the big set moved in various ways, depending on the segment of the show. Although the stage was enormous, 70,000 people is a massive audience; as is customary these days, giant video screens flanked the hefty banks of mammoth loudspeakers on either side of the staging.

In Leeds, Madonna first appeared near the top of the main flight of steps, silhouetted against the backdrop, relaxed languidly on a chair for all the world, like a nightclub hostess lazily about to get going. In London, sometimes she appeared cheekily from behind one of the screens, after a brilliantly vivid flash of light, right across the arena, momentarily blinded the onlookers, and immediately got the show off to a cracking start.

Neither Wembley or Roundhay could be considered really suitable for relayed music, with pockets of echo and awkwardly bouncing terraces, uncertain surrebounding chasms of sound, and other attendant problems. But the sound engineers overcame the problems magnificently, and when the band broke into the opening bars of 'Open Your Heart', the aural aspect of the show matched the visual one perfectly. A great deal of hard work and skill had gone into this staging – anyone could see and hear that. Before the show proper had begun, the audience caught a glimpse of a real live toy-boy – fourteen-year-old Chris Finch, a talented and handsome young Californian. Then Madonna came down the stairs and pranced provocatively from left to right and back again. She wore a black bodice with tights and boots with short socks. She called out: 'It's cold up here but I want us to keep each other warm. Don't touch the person next to you, or I'll maybe get jealous.' 'Open Your Heart', the first number, set the mood, and little by little the Madonna choreographic routine built up: a sudden jump here, a flash of semi-splits there, a suggestion of break-dancing, then Chris Finch returned, a brilliantly gifted dancer. After his routine, he sat down on the chair and Madonna spoke briefly to the audience before going into her 'lucky song', 'Lucky Star'. She was getting closer to the audience in more ways that one: flirting, and oozing sexuality as she slid over the floor, suggestively calling 'come on' again and again.

Suddenly, she disappeared to return minutes later wearing a frilly pale blue dress and chiffon scarf for 'True Blue' – no longer

109

the stripper at a seedy joint, but a presentable party-goer for every generation. The backing girl singers – previously either only heard, or glimpsed at briefly from a distance – were now fully, deliberately, visible. The startling string-orchestral introduction to 'Papa Don't Preach' immediately had the audience clapping expectantly. Madonna donned a leather jacket over her frilly dress and at once her style was more urban, as she slowly paced the stage. At the words 'I'm keeping my baby' she clutched her stomach for a fraction of a second, all the while accompanied by startling visual images – often political (America in the 1960s, the Kennedys) or religious (Pope John Paul II) or genuinely tragic (Robert Kennedy shot, oozing blood on the kitchen floor at the Ambassador Hotel in Los Angeles). The strongest, most apposite message was left to last, a massive 'SAFE SEX' lingering on the screen after the music had ended, no doubt in memory of Martin Burgoyne.

While the opening strains of 'White Heat' were playing and the video was showing Chicago in the 1930s, Madonna disappeared for another quick change and came back wearing a long gold coat and gangster-style hat and holding a gun, with which she shot a trio of 'gangsters'. Chris Finch returned, throwing himself into a spectacular series of cartwheels during the next song, 'Causing A Commotion', with Madonna playing a false guitar; still wearing the gold top-coat, Madonna changed the tempo for 'The Look of Love', strolling at a slow pace. But in 'Dress You Up' she made a humorous entrance from a traditional Post Office red telephone box, the type that is now rare in Britain, and wearing spoof 'fashion' spectacles with a Mad Hatter-style red topper decorated with fruit and flowers. Her red dress also glanced at the nineteenth century: a bodice atop a crinoline-suggestive almost-mini skirt which was festooned with all kinds of paraphernalia – cheap plastic jewellery, false eyes on coiled springs, large 'car-rear-window' dice, fashion erasers, Christmas-cracker 'novelties', bunches of plastic grapes and much else besides, all done in a bizarre tapestry.

Next the screen was illuminated with a large dollar sign: the 'Material Girl' had arrived and money was the object. This was choreographed as an extended set-piece between Madonna and two dancers, Angel and Shabba Doo, the latter suffering from a badly kicked collar-bone, accidentally inflicted by Madonna during the first Wembley rehearsal. Towards the end of the song,

'Madonna-money' was distributed before the final eye-blinking event – Madonna removed her knickers and threw them into the audience, virtually causing a stampede.

After that she slipped off her outer-clothes to reveal a sexy dark-blue leotard edged with gold piping. Chris Finch returned to join Madonna in an Astaire-Rogers-style display to the song, 'Like a Virgin', which ended in a stylized embrace, with Chris's left leg shaking like an extended branch in mid-air as Madonna kissed him full on the lips.

The next outfit featured midnight-blue trousers and a feather boa, and some masked-ball-style black spectacles, for 'Where's The Party?'. Then the tempo slowed for 'Live To Tell', the Martin Burgoyne tribute. There was a quiet moment after that song then a complete change of mood as Madonna threw on a tasselled and studded black leather jacket and yelled to the audience, 'Can you dance?' There followed an extended remix version of 'Into The Groove' then Madonna left the stage. This was supposed to be the end of the concert but none of the audiences would let her go and after a short wait she re-appeared for the first encore, wearing a dazzling flamenco-style flame-red dress with matador top, garnished with sequins, to sing 'La Isla Bonita'. She then moved into 'Who's That Girl?' after seventy minutes which had fully demonstrated all of her remarkable gifts – as singer, songwriter, dancer, choreographer, actress and crowd-puller.

At the end of this song, the lights were gradually extinguished and people were beginning to gather up their possessions ready to leave when the lights came back on and Madonna bounced back wearing a red jumpsuit, bopping away to 'Holiday'. Then, eventually, it really was over, and the audience filed out, still glancing back over their shoulders to see if there were any more surprises to come.

Overall it was a very up-lifting show, demonstrating a positive attitude to life. The image of Madonna was of someone saying 'Yes' to fun and 'Yes' to sex and basically enjoying life to the full despite some moments of introspection.

The tour, begun in Japan, and continued in America and Europe, with appearances in France, Holland, West Germany and Italy, demonstrated that her appeal was truly worldwide. While in Italy, playing concerts in Turin, Florence and Rome, she made a sentimental journey to Pacentro, near Florence, the birthplace of her grandparents, where scores of her distant relatives still live. The event was recorded for Italian television and issued on video.

In France, where her concert in Sceaux, a Parisian suburb south of the city, was scheduled, no less a person than the French Prime Minister, M Jacques Chirac, took a hand in ensuring the concert went ahead after the local mayor threatened to ban it, claiming that the visit would be too great a threat to public order. With 100,000 fans to be controlled by 1,500 riot police, the mayor had a point, but M Chirac's twenty-four-year-old daughter was an avid Madonna fan. When she heard of the mayor's decision, she waylaid her father and persuaded him to use his influence to get the ban lifted, which he did. M Chirac, subjected to a crash-course in Madonna-mania by his daughter, went on to describe the singer as a 'great and beautiful artist'.

Furthermore, M Chirac laid on a reception at Paris City Hall, and arranged for his family to meet Madonna in private before the concert; in return, Madonna presented him with a cheque for 500,000 francs, a donation to Aids research in France. The mayor of Sceaux, now brought into line by the political power of popular music's appeal, claimed he would do 'all he could to make the concert take place in the best possible conditions'.

Finally at the beginning of October, the tour was over, and an exhausted Madonna returned home to Sean and to recover from a highly punishing schedule. 'After the *Who's That Girl?* tour I said to myself, "I don't ever want to hear any of my songs ever again and I don't know whether I'll ever write another one." I returned feeling so burned out and I was convinced I wouldn't go near music for quite a while. But Pat Leonard built this new studio and I went to see it – within an hour we'd written this great song. It amazed me.'

The success of the world tour had spin-offs in other directions, some of them unwelcome. The merchandizing sales were vast, her record sales reached all-time levels, but *Penthouse* magazine ran an issue containing more of the nude modelling poses of seven or eight years previously. Her fame and international acceptance were such that their publication came and went virtually unnoticed. However, the tour had generated such enormous interest that it had to be satisfied and capitalized upon by a new release, and taking her roots, the dance floor, and the best of her dance material, Sire Records brilliantly timed the worldwide release of the *You Can Dance* album,

Previous page, Who *is* that girl? *Above,* Madonna and her husband Sean Penn visiting the office of her Hollwyood agent. *Below,* Avoiding the paparazzi, Sean makes clear his feelings as they attempt to leave a restaurant parking lot after a quiet dinner.

Left and Below, Mr and Mrs Sean Penn, in happier days.

Right, Madonna and her bodyguard, Clay Tave, at the AIDS project, Los Angeles 'Commitment to Life' in 1986. *Below,* Madonna as Gloria Tatlock in *Shanghai Surprise.*

Right, Madonna accepts an award at the American MTV awards in 1986. *Below,* Madonna poses for photographers at the 14th annual American Music Awards in 1987, just previous to the release of 'Who's That Girl?'.

Left, Newly slimmed and full of life, Madonna entrances the audience on her 1987 'Who's That Girl?' tour.

Right, Pausing mid-song, Madonna sports her brother's extravagant creation during her 1987 tour.

Above, Driving herself home after dinner at her favourite restaurant in Beverly Hills. *Left,* Leaving the theatre following a Broadway performance of *Speed the Plow.* *Overleaf, left,* Madonna at a benefit to save the rainforests, May 1989. *Overleaf, right,* Madonna jogging *sans* minders in New York's Central Park.

for November 1987, an album of previously unreleased and newly remixed versions of her best dance material.

This was not, of itself, a new idea in the record business, but whereas some earlier examples had been little more than cut-up redubs, this was little short of a triumph for all involved. Chris Heath, reviewing the album for *Smash Hits* magazine, said of the release that it 'is rather wonderful. It's especially good because most of the songs are from the early part of Madonna's career – back when she was covered with crucifixes, never combed her hair . . . and it includes the two best songs she ever made . . . they're messed around just enough to make them exciting all over again'.

The release of this total dance album towards the end of 1987 was an excellent attempt to show Madonna's roots and how they could be back-translated from the charts into the basis of her art. Rare among dance-chart success artists, Madonna has been able to cross over into the national charts: the *You Can Dance* album is her first retrospective, what would have been termed in earlier years as her 'Greatest Hits' album. *You Can Dance* is, in many ways, just that, but each track has been remixed by a top disc-jockey to make it not only longer but also a different listening experience.

'Spotlight' begins the album, and is notable for a subtle overlaying of dance percussion in the extended instrumental sequence by Jellybean Benitez; it slides effortlessly into 'Holiday', with which it always had a family connection – the two hook lines of the titles being set to adjacent chords. This was also remixed by Jellybean, although he claimed the original was dance-oriented in the first place and that it needed very little in the way of remixing, apart from adding a very few new sounds four years after the original 1983 version.

'Everybody' also seems to have little added to it by Bruce Forest apart from keyboards by David Cole – Forest has reported that this classic dance track has never gone out of style in his 'Better Days' New York club, and there was quite clearly no need for him to have done a major job of recomposition on what was already one of the definitive tracks, but there is occasionally a curious impression of a slower time-speed being used, as though the original and the remix do not quite gel together.

As 'Everybody' fades, it is cross-phased with the introduction from 'Physical Attraction', originally produced by Reggie Lucas

113

and interpolated here before the dub version of 'Spotlight', an extended version that adds a little more to our knowledge of it – including a totally unexpected and superb ending, an a capella-style chord leaving the song hanging in mid-air. This dub version is only available on the cassette version, and is followed by the dub version of 'Holiday', which is on all formats and which brings side one to a close.

The beginning of side two is 'Over and Over', remixed by Steve Thompson and Michael Barbiero. There was little wrong with the original production by Nile Rodgers, but the new keyboard tracks by Jack Waldman and Jimmy Maelen's additional percussion are masterfully dovetailed into the original tape to produce a wholly unexpected and convincing view of the track. Steve Thompson recalled Maelen's work, as he 'really wailed, playing live percussion to a machine drum track'.

'Into The Groove' was remixed by Shep Pettibone, with an extensive amount of overdubbing but carried out with such style and musicianship that Madonna herself now prefers to perform this version rather than the earlier one. The over-dub at the beginning of the second main section heralds a new sound-world and major surgery on the original track, but again it is exceptionally well done, and is made golden by the astonishing solo piano break played by the session engineer, Andy Wallace, who – as Pettibone recalled – 'just started and was really inspired. I had no idea what he'd play.'

After these two outstanding tracks – which between them justify the album's existence as nothing else does – 'Where's The Party?' moulds excellently into the sound-frame, also mixed by Shep Pettibone. The dub version of 'Over and Over' returns (another track only available on the cassette edition) with Madonna's voice judged with layers of post-echo as befits the title, until finally 'Into The Groove' pulls the album to a close with jangly-dangly keyboards – the whole exercise forming a remarkable and possibly unique type of release, issued not just in the wake of the *'Who's That Girl?'* Tour, but as a valid and interesting adjunct to her work up to that time and a very convincing demonstration of the best in dance remix for leisure listening. The album was sequenced by Jellybean, and listening to it overall it is difficult to imagine how it could have been better done.

The release of Madonna's *You Can Dance* album in November

1987 would seem to have brought an astonishing year for her to a close. But she was not yet finished. Her charitable work took a new turn with the recording and release of a Christmas song, 'Santa Baby', the proceeds from which were to be donated to charities for disabled people. 'Santa Baby' is not, in truth, her finest recording: the song is faintly innocuous and has to be listened to with a certain amount of indulgence, but it fits the bill and catches the Christmas spirit admirably. The amount of money she had raised for different charities during the year was quite exceptional – with her work for Aids charities and hospitals, her Live Aid appearance, and now a single to benefit the disabled.

11

LIKE A PRAYER

Madonna's exertions during the previous year or so demanded a rest. At the turn of the year she let it be known that she was taking a long period away from music. But this would not be an enforced idleness; she formed a new company, Siren Films, to indicate the direction which her career was now likely to take. Thus far, Siren Films has yet to bring its first results before the public: the important thing is that, as far as her screen career is concerned, she regards it as her highest priority for the future.

In the early months of 1988, Madonna began work on a Warner Brothers project, a remake of the 1952 film *Bloodhounds of Broadway* which had originally featured Mitzi Gaynor and Mitzi Green. Madonna starred with Jennifer Grey, who had had a great success in *Dirty Dancing*, and with Matt Dillon, as a gangster with good intentions. The story by Damon Runyan was originally described by Leslie Halliwell as an 'absurd, but sporadically amusing gangster burlesque', and is set in New York in the Prohibition 1920s. Over a year after it was made, *Bloodhounds of Broadway* has not seen the light of day and details of it are very sketchy; rumours abound that the result was not up to expectations and the film may possibly appear either on television or as a video-only release. Madonna has not referred to it publicly.

Of all the modern-day stars of the music and screen world Madonna seems to be one of the most stable and intelligent. Even her detractors admit that she possesses an enormous capacity for hard work, an inner drive that enables her to accomplish a great deal, and that drugs form no part of her stimulation. 'I have my moments of exhaustion, but I can go for nights without sleeping

116

if I'm not working on anything specifically. If I'm doing a tour or working on a film I really have to be on the ball so I make sure I get to bed early. I need at least six hours sleep so I have to cut down on my social life if I want to feel good the next day. When occasionally I get eight hours sleep I find it hard to believe.

'I like to have control over most of the things in my career but I'm not a tyrant. I don't have to have it on my albums that it's written, produced, directed and stars Madonna. To me, to have total control means you can lose objectivity. What I like is to be surrounded by really talented, intelligent people you can trust. And ask them for their advice and get their input. But let's face it, I'm not going to make an album and not show up for the vocals or make a video and have nothing to do with the script.'

We have seen how difficult it has been for Sean Penn to come to terms with the staggering amount of press interest his marriage to Madonna has generated. He had often been publicly baited beyond endurance. He had literally been to jail over her; the experience, however well-treated he was by the authorities, could only have been a humbling and humiliating one for him. As a founder-member of the Hollywood 'brat pack' Sean's reputation for being a hard-drinking, brawling young man may have been exaggerated, but it would have stood him in little stead in a courtroom, charged with assault and other misdemeanours. The incarceration and the enforced separation from his wife during her world tour made him reappraise his situation. He loved Madonna – no doubt about that – and she him, equally. But no couple can be expected to live their lives successfully under such perpetual strain.

The strains upon their marriage were complicated by a particularly unpleasant event early in 1988: their home in Malibu was broken into by a so-called 'superfan', who prowled around, frightening Madonna, albeit momentarily, but reminding them both of the risks their individual and combined fame had brought. Unless either of them wanted to become a recluse, thereby cutting themselves off from what passes as the real world, such unpleasantness had to be accepted as a fact of life. In an attempt to return to a reasonably 'normal' life after the virtual six months of world touring, Madonna took the courageous step of flying by herself from Los Angeles to New York – a simple enough matter for most people but unheard-of for a star who employed minders and bodyguards. She enjoyed the flight:

sitting next to just another passenger, and willingly signing the many autographs she was asked to give once she had been recognized; such a straightforward experience came as a welcome breather for her. 'It was the first time I'd done anything like that in a long time because I usually travel with my secretary or some kind of security person. I was so frightened. People are crazy and they think they know you and they won't leave you alone. But I ended up sitting next to a very nice guy in advertising. He knew who I was because people kept coming up for autographs. It's healthy for me to force myself to move about independently. It helps me to touch base with reality. I could never live a sheltered life. That would drive me insane.'

The reason for her trip to New York was a professional one. We have seen how anxious she was to become accepted as an actress, and a serious actress at that. Her film company was a first step in that direction, but a more significant one, by far, was her auditioning for a part in a new Broadway play, *Speed The Plough* by David Mamet. Together with around thirty other actresses, she auditioned by reading sections of the part of Karen, the only female part in the three-handed play. Mamet was very impressed with Madonna, saying she had read beautifully, and she got the role.

The month was marred somewhat by a charge brought against Madonna's eighteen-year-old brother Mario, alleging he smashed a door in the face of a policeman during a party in Detroit, but the news of her imminent Broadway appearance brushed all unpleasantness aside for the time being. Scheduled to open at the Royale Theatre within a matter of weeks, David Mamet's three-acter dealt with modern morals in Tinseltown.

In *Speed the Plow* Madonna, as Karen, played a temporary secretary, sent to cover for the currently ill permanent secretary of a head of a Hollywood production company (a guy named Gould, played by Joe Mantegna) who bets his assistant, played by the fashionably designer-stubbled Ron Silver, $500 that he can seduce Karen. In the event, near the beginning of Act Two, when she arrives at his home that evening (ostensibly to deliver a book report as instructed) Gould feels he has virtually won his bet, but instead of slipping into bed with him, Karen delivers a few well-chosen words on the sort of films he ought to be making. Gould is taken aback – firstly, because her attitude is not what he was expecting, and secondly because she reveals that she knew about the bet and came, nevertheless, as she wanted to know how he would go about it and she found him not at all unattractive into the bargain.

The director of the play, Gregory Mosher, spoke of Madonna's audition as 'decisive', and went on to comment, in an interview with the New York *Daily News*, that 'you cannot take your eyes off her when she is on stage. It's scary how much talent she has.'

Once accepted for the part, Madonna buckled down to a strict new regimen, a punishing physical schedule as demanding as she had undertaken the previous year in preparation for the *'Who's That Girl?'* tour. She also abandoned meat-eating, becoming a strict vegan and losing some weight in the process. *Speed the Plough* opened during the first week of May 1988, and advance bookings were enough to ensure a reasonable profit for the backers. It soon came to be known as 'The Madonna Play,' for many had booked seats just to see how the same girl – spunkily touring the world eight months previously in her own amazing rock show – would transfer to the rigorous intellectual demands of a major part in a serious Broadway drama. The reaction from the 'critics' of certain sections of the press was utterly predictable, but those more restrained and experienced in their judgment were undoubtedly impressed. One of these, the distinguished Broadway critic for *The Guardian*, W J Weatherby, said, 'Madonna fans, made up in the style of the superstar singer for her concerts, were already waiting outside the stage door of the Royale Theatre when the curtain went up on her Broadway debut. Security was so heavy inside the theatre that a member of the audience who had the temerity to leave his seat in the middle of an over-long first act was followed and interrogated.

'At least the audience did not cheer Madonna's entrance. That was probably because they did not recognize her. In place of her usual glamorously aggressive style, she had a modest businesslike appearance with her hair dyed reddish brown and sedately trimmed, and dressed in conventional, if figure-hugging office clothes . . . [Karen] admitting at the outset that she has no idea what to do. "Naïve" is a key word. She is naïve in much the same way as the late Marilyn Monroe – with an underlying honesty and shrewdness about the world. Madonna, in fact, is playing what looks like Mamet's version of the early Marilyn (who also had an ambition to star on Broadway) . . . Mamet with his tape-recorder ear for dialogue has a great time mocking the slick Hollywood banter and sexual jokes, and he plays a paradoxical game worthy of Bernard Shaw in making the naïve "temporary girl's" innocence outsmart the worldliness of the Hollywood boss.

'*Speed the Plough* must be taken on its own terms as an amusing if occasionally overlong contemporary American fable. It is probably as far as Madonna, if not Mamet himself, can go in the theatre. The singer's fans may be disappointed by her disciplined self-restraint, but that is precisely the measure of her achievement . . . Instead of the usual Hollywood luxury, the economical settings convey a run-down wasteland. I hope that was the intention rather than the effect of a low-budget production. At least it serves to further de-glamorize Madonna.'

The de-glamorizing, probably intentional after the mega-stardom of the previous year was helped by dissenting reviews, notably those from CBS's Broadway theatre critic: 'Her ineptitude is scandalously thorough . . . She cannot give meaning to the words she is saying. I've never seen on a Broadway stage someone who didn't have the basic elements of acting.' The *Daily News* also demurred from W J Weatherby's view: 'Elegantly designed, impeccably directed, *Speed-the-Plow* is Mamet's clearest, wittiest, play. I bet it would be even funnier with an actress.' But the *New York Times* shared the opinions of the more respected and regular theatre critics, when the newspaper's correspondent found her performance to be made up of 'intelligent, scrupulously disciplined comic acting'.

The novelist Harry Crews, who also interviewed Madonna towards the end of 1988, found that he greatly admired 'David Mamet's work, but *Speed-The-Plow* is badly flawed. Madonna's is the pivotal role, and her character makes less dramatic sense than does the play. But I thought her exceptional, given what she had to work with.'

We have some chance of deciding for ourselves, as a video has been issued of a fairly sizeable portion of the play featuring Madonna, and including comments on her performance from Jennifer Gray and Billy Joel. But whatever the final view, Madonna's six-month nightly stint on Broadway provided her with the perfect antidote to the excesses of the world tour. It also provided her with a single-minded project which would stand her in very good stead in the future. She was able to use the Broadway run as a base from which she could explore various avenues without having to concern herself too much with a 'public image' (impossible to change or develop as she had to appear the same almost every night of the week). Precisely because of the straight-jacketing effect of acting the same role every evening, her daily work could take the form of planning and of being very much behind the scenes of new projects.

Once the play was up and running, Madonna soon busied herself with a number of musical ideas. She wrote a song for Marilyn Martin, who has a voice not unlike Madonna's, called 'Possessive Love' and recorded it, producing the single for her in New York in May. Two months later, she again appeared in the recording studio, singing backing vocals for her new Nick Kamen single, 'Tell Me', but this time she was not the producer.

Ideas had been buzzing around for a new album for some time, but she herself explained how she regarded her approach to the essential difference between her concert and her serious acting. 'On the road doing my own show everything changes every day – different city, different feel for the audience because the people are always different wherever you go – and there's always something new to pique your interest. Plus it's *my* show. I can take great liberties and change whatever I want. I can't do that here [at the Royale Theatre]. I'm interpreting somebody else's work in the same theatre at the same time every night on 45th Street.'

But the new discipline, the new experience and knowledge Madonna gained during the Broadway run were not acquired without having to pay some unwelcome prices. At the beginning of July, Sean had returned to their New York home after filming *Casualties of War* in Thailand, and was reunited with Madonna for only the second time in four months, having escorted her to the Spinks-Tyson World Heavyweight Championship fight – a ninety-one-second demolition job by the champion Tyson – which had taken place a few days previously on 28 June.

They were walking near their Central Park home when Paul Adao, a New York photographer, somehow got embroiled with Sean while taking snaps of them. Adao called a passing policeman and Sean – still on probation after his first assault case the previous year – was arrested. Madonna herself was approached by a fan with a camera on another occasion whilst walking home and she let off a stream of abuse at the youth, hitting him and ripping the camera from his neck. A year later, she was awaiting the legal outcome of her own fracas.

A few days after the trouble on the street with Paul Adao, Madonna's friendship with the lesbian comedienne Sandra Bernhard became public knowledge. Having seen her one-woman show, which included a sketch featuring Madonna and Sean at home, Madonna went backstage to compliment her and a firm friendship developed. They were guests on the same David Letterman show and professed their love for each other, with Sandra raising the programme's temperature several degrees by claiming that she had slept with Sean, but that Madonna was much better. Whilst it was pretty obvious that the chat-show exchange was very much tongue-in-cheek, some commentators went overboard in their claims that Madonna had had a lesbian relationship with Sandra. Whatever the truth of the matter, Madonna's open friendship with Sandra Bernhard hardly helped her battered relationship with Sean.

On 1 July 1988 it was announced that Madonna had beaten Greta Scacchi and Barbara Streisand to land the role of Evita in the film of the musical; some weeks later, it was learned the plans had been terminated, to be replaced by a claim that she was anxious to play the part of Tiger Lily in the forthcoming Peter Pan movie. That, also, remained an unfulfilled project. But her success in *Speed The Plough* had undoubtedly borne fruit in her acting career: new film projects were offered, some considered, some accepted subject to commitments, and some declined. There could be no doubt that – the comments of some critics notwithstanding – she was now accepted as a genuine actress, and very much so by some notable Hollywood stars.

The run of the play came to its allotted end in November 1988, and Madonna could spend some time with her family at Thanksgiving, and with Sean. But her marriage, which had survived a succession of tempestuous arguments and fractures, split beyond repair just after Christmas. The couple had begun the holiday at their Malibu home with several house-guests, including Sandra Bernhard. On Year's Eve, Sean had allegedly drunk more than was good for him and an argument developed. She claimed that during the course of this argument Sean had physically attacked her and then left her bound and gagged, until she was freed by her staff at 1 a.m on New Year's Day after nine hours. A secretary is reported to have claimed that the event was 'the final degradation after three years of hell. Madonna was weeping. Her lip was bleeding, her spirit was crushed. She was marked and sore where he had cracked her across the face.'

The tension had been building up for some time; he had confessed during December 1988 that he had a drink problem which was seriously affecting his marriage. Sean spent much of the Christmas holiday period at his parents' home, further upset at Sandra Bernhard's presence at their Malibu home, and it has been alleged that he crept back to the house, through the wooded grounds, and broke in through a rear door. The police were called and they confirm that 'a peripheral involvement' had occurred at the house, but declined further comment. The following day, 2 January, Madonna telephoned her lawyers telling them to file for divorce from Sean at Santa Monica District Court, reportedly saying 'That's it. File for a divorce now. I can't take any more.' She told her staff: 'Sandra's going. I will face this alone.' The papers were deposited with the Court on 5 January. Her staff were required to provide sworn statements regarding the events at the mansion on the night of 31 December. Under recently enacted Californian divorce law, no matter who was the 'guilty party' of a divorce action, each partner is entitled to half of the combined wealth of the couple, and Madonna was undoubtedly much wealthier than her husband. But Sean is reported to have said to her, 'I'll go and I won't take one stinking cent. You can have it all.'

So a marriage, which had lasted for over three years, came to a bitter and acrimonious end. However, Madonna now refuses to confirm those early reports of events of New Year's Eve, although the divorce proceedings are going ahead. When questioned about it, she described the reports as 'extremely inaccurate, as they usually are. They made it all up. But I expect it. They're always making things up.' Allowing for the exaggeration of some newshounds, the fact remains that she did call the Malibu Police Department to her home that evening to investigate her complaint, although she subsequently withdrew the charges.

The break-up could not have been entirely one-sided; as Madonna herself said earlier: 'I guess a lot of my hot-blooded and passionate temperament is Italian . . . Italian men like to dominate and sometimes I like to cast myself in the submissive role.' She further explains that she had been guilty of not speaking out about her own needs in the relationship: 'Sometimes you feel that if you ask for too much or ask for the wrong thing from somebody you care about, then that person won't like you.' And it is obvious that she had been unable to give Sean the support that he needed in his very demanding career because a lot of the time she could not physically be there, given her other commitments.

Madonna's Italian temperament and Catholic upbringing must have made it even more difficult and traumatic for her to walk away from her marriage. Although it is dangerous to read too much into an artist's work and apply it to their lives, the themes of the *Like A Prayer* album, to which she was putting the finishing touches in January 1989, reflect her situation and maybe helped her to work out some of her sadness.

Like A Prayer was released on 20 March 1989, two weeks after the title single. For an artist whose last release was almost eighteen months previously, the fact that in the United Kingdom the single went straight in at the top of the charts – and the album likewise – and remained there for a month, was incredible. But much of what Madonna had achieved during her life had been unprecedented, and the nature of her achievement in this instance was also unique. A deal had been struck with the giant multi-national soft drinks company, Pepsi-Cola, after eight months of tough three-way negotiations between Pepsi, Sire Records and Madonna, in which Madonna would appear in a long (more than two-minutes' duration) commercial to advertise Pepsi-Cola, the music for which would be the title track from the new album. The company's use of a major star to promote their product was by no means a new departure for Pepsi: they had previously engaged Michael Jackson, Tina Turner, David Bowie, Lionel Richie, the Miami Sound Machine, Michael J. Fox and Mike Tyson. But the difference with the Madonna involvement was the extent of Pepsi's promotion of her. Not only was this a worldwide deal, with the television ad showing throughout forty countries on the same night – a massive trans-continental advertising media buy – but also the most comprehensive sponsored promotion yet achieved for popular music, for the company's involvement with Madonna extended to sponsorship of a new world tour which was still being planned at that stage. Although the Michael Jackson *Bad* tour had been

Pepsi-sponsored (being particularly successful for the company in Japan) and one of his commercials had become so popular that it was listed in the TV sections of American newspapers so that viewers knew when to tune in, the worldwide Madonna launch on the same night had never been attempted before. It was the first time a new single had been unveiled in this way. This was somewhat of a gamble for Pepsi, as their financial involvement was very deep. Madonna was reputedly being paid around five million dollars for the ad (about three million pounds), and the tour sponsorship would be far in excess of that figure. The media bookings alone added millions more.

Pepsi had created a 'teaser' commercial for the actual commercial, which previewed on 24 February. In the teaser ad, a young aborigine treks across the Australian Outback until he reaches his destination – a lone café, which possesses a satellite television receiving dish – to watch the Madonna ad. The teaser contains shots of Madonna preparing to film the commercial, which was made on location in Arizona by the legendary Joe Pytka, who had directed the company's earlier ads with Michael Jackson. Entitled 'Make a Wish', the ad itself was a brilliant combination of elements: it opens with videos of her early life: a childhood birthday party, her Catholic schooling – whilst actually dancing in a black Baptist church – with early appearances and so on, ending with a return to the birthday party, at which a happy, six-year-old Madonna half turns to the camera to smile, holding a can of Pepsi. Smiling back at the screen, the adult Madonna raises her can to toast her childhood self. And throughout this ad, which is compulsive viewing, we hear the new 'Like A Prayer' single, the whole campaign forming part of Pepsi's on-going 'Taste of America' promotional strategy in the USA.

It is one thing to have such successfully organized support: with that kind of exposure, almost anything would have been catapulted into the best-selling lists. But it is quite another thing to stay there, dominating the world's popular record sales, week after week, with the ad only being shown once in Britain and twice in the USA. Another video had been made to accompany the single and in terms of publicity this also had a massive, worldwide impact, but perhaps not in quite the way everyone had hoped.

'Like A Prayer' is a song about a young girl with a crush on God. The video depicts a girl witnessing an assault in the street then seeing a black man falsely arrested. One of the gang members has seen her so she is too scared to intervene and she runs to a church for sanctuary where she sees a saint in a cage who looks like the black man in the street. She starts to pray and a dream sequence follows in which a woman saves her from falling and tells her to do the right thing. The saint stirs her religious and erotic feelings and guiltily she cuts her hand with a knife. The dancing reaches a crescendo and when she wakes up she goes to jail, tells the police everything and the black man is freed. The video ends with the cast taking a bow, as if at the end of a play.

The moral majority immediately leapt upon it as blasphemous, as Madonna making love with a saint – some thought it was Jesus Christ himself. The American Family Association in particular denounced it as offensive and, although it had been made for television, few US TV companies would actually show it. Madonna shrugged off their reaction, claiming that 'Art should be controversial and that's all there is to it.' But events went further than she had expected. The furore over her video coincided with the worldwide Muslim outcry over Salman Rushdie's novel *Satanic Verses*, which ended with the author going into hiding as he was condemned to death by the Ayatollah Khomeini. The Islamic Organization for Media Monitoring claimed that Madonna's video was blasphemous, since it insulted Jesus Christ, regarded as a prophet in Islamic belief. The punishment for insulting a prophet under traditional Islamic law is death.

All the critics appear to have missed the point that in the video Madonna is a believer. There is a mixture of sacred and profane images – of stigmata and burning crosses, recalling the Klu Klux Klan's persecution of black people – but the overall message is one of Christianity and treating all races as equal.

As the uproar continued, Pepsi were drawn into the fray with religious groups threatening a boycott of their product in the United States and drink dispensers being removed from the recreation rooms of Catholic schools; thousands of complaints were received from members of the public and from religious leaders, and eventually Pepsi were forced to break off their contract with Madonna and withdraw their adverts. The decision about whether they will withdraw their sponsorship of the Madonna world tour, starting in September 1989, has been deferred.

Meanwhile, the *Like A Prayer* album shows a new mature Madonna at the peak of her creative powers. It begins with the title song. A crescendo of tunnelling white noise shatters the silence: a sharp chord catches the attention, then Madonna slowly intones the opening lines of the song. The words are clearly meant to be heard, for no backing music can blur them. A slow-dance rhythm starts but is interrupted for a celestial couplet, Madonna's voice now silhouetted against a wordless female choir. This is a double exposition: gradually male voices enter to support her. Once more the process is gone through, the choir now with Madonna, who occasionally duets in harmony with herself. This may seem a curious beginning to a pop song; and indeed it is, but 'Like a Prayer' encompasses a long time-scale. The rhythm knocks the song's rhythmic engine into life and continues through the rest of the number, with Madonna's voice lower and more expressive here than we seem to remember. The rhythmic drumming is soft but insistent, and there is an imaginative use of stereo as she ascends, ethereally, into the sky to echo the chanting chorus.

A great drum richochet brings us to the present. 'Express yourself' is now, vividly today, the contrast between it and the opening number being quite marked. Aurally, the song has a tighter acoustic feel to it, concentrating the mind on its faster, more urgent, elements. This exuberant, catchy and funky number, with a shade of Four Seasons added for spice, is a plea for a couple to talk more if they're in trouble. It became the second single to be released from the album and a very erotic video was made to accompany it, with some brilliant dance sequences and a glimpse of Madonna pouring milk over her breasts.

A detour is undertaken with the third number, an extraordinary 'Love Song' sung in duet with Prince. The bass line is predominant here, the tempo slow, in a Sly and the Family Stone side-1-track-3-manner. The song begins with some gently spoken Madonna French, but the continental influence ends there. Their duet is startlingly original: musically, it spins gently off-key, like a mind recovering from a bad experience, trying to hang on to reality. Surprisingly, Madonna and Prince's voices blend with a fine degree of harmoniousness, and the production is impressive. Madonna has commented that she always wanted to work with Prince, for whom she has the greatest admiration, but seemingly their schedules were such that they had to create this track by post, sending the tape backwards and forwards as they added new bits.

'Till Death Us Do Part' is a fast, jumpy song, seemingly unwilling to ponder over the unusually deep lyrics. It's about a marriage full of drunken, violent quarrels from which neither partner can escape. The subject changes from the first person to the third, almost as though the idea has become too unbearable to contemplate. These lyrics must relate to the break up of Madonna's marriage, and the length of the song – another five-minutes-plus number – indicates the obsession with the subject matter. The music breaks up, momentarily fragments and dissolves into speech for the title line, before it returns, blandly smoothing away the hurt.

The fifth song, 'Promise To Try', drops the tempo right down and is possibly the slowest song Madonna has ever recorded. The extraordinary instrumentation: solo piano (sensitively played by the song's co-writer Pat Leonard) with string orchestra and a superb cello solo by Larry Corbett, places this very much on a serious plane. The song meanders sadly, as the singer imagines her mother observing her as a little girl and offering advice and support. Worlds away from the chirpy 'Holiday', this shows a depth of feeling, a new side to Madonna which must surely blow away any remaining doubts about her musical ability.

The line 'So tired of broken hearts' begins 'Cherish', and at first we might think this is another downbeat piece of autobiographical writing. It is not; here Madonna is thinking of a new love, one to 'cherish', but a special one. It is a bouncy, three-minute dance number, with the lyrics of a serious love song – a combination we have had from her before, with such earlier songs as 'Wrap You Up'. There is an unexpected break into a cappella near the end of this cheerful number.

The string-orchestral opening to 'True Blue' is recalled in 'Dear Jessie', a layered string texture with backing percussion. So fascinating is the instrumentation that it almost detracts from the words, which have a neo-psychedelic Beatles-style charm, concerning leprechauns, merry-go-rounds, mermaids singing, and someone who can make dreams come true. The orchestra fades into a pre-war three-inch radio speaker, collapsing like a crumbling miniature by Webern.

In 'Oh Father' the singer berates a cruel father figure/husband/religious authority. Madonna has referred to this song as being influenced by Simon and Garfunkel. The line 'O Father, I have sinned' recalls a 'rosary' but other lines are more down to earth. It's about breaking away from someone who has the power to hurt you and although the singer claims to have escaped, the mournful tone belies it.

'Keep it Together' is a song about a kid who wants to escape from the restraints of family life but whose father urges him/her to stay because strength comes from the family. Brothers and sisters are the people that you can turn to in times of need, when you are lonely and need people who will see you for what you are and not what they want you to be. This is not the best song on the album but the lyrics are interesting in the light of Madonna's personal circumstances at the time.

The tenth song, 'Spanish Eyes' (not the Al Martino hit of the early 1970s), flickers across the loudspeaker with an acoustic Spanish guitar line, gently tracing over the soft-beat background and the restrained use of percussion. A slow tango, with Tijuana brass weaving far in the background, and this is revealed as a song for the Hispanics in America, now more than 15 per cent of the population, a Catholic minority not always accorded their civil rights. The song is enigmatic, personal, private, a call to a fellow-army of 'fighters' and to Christ and God for help and compassion.

And finally a whispering, blaring catharsis, a witty mélange of tape-loops, spoken prayers, gospel songs, a funky dancing confessional, a penitential Act of Contrition, ending and underlining the Catholic themes which have formed a basis for so much of the material on this album, entitled *Like A Prayer* and written and performed by a woman named 'Madonna'.

This album finally proves that, artistically, she needs no-one else. She is there, triumphant, amazing and continuing to demonstrate, along with other major artists, that popular music is worthwhile, is important, is valid entirely in its own terms. It hit the charts within days of its release in March 1989 with the force of a detonation. Reviewers were almost unanimously enthusiastic, commenting on her maturing as an artist and the depth and quality of the material. *New Musical Express*, for example, called it 'a brilliant, thoughtful, startling and joyful example of popular music' and commented

that it showed 'obvious signs of post-divorce rethinking and con-
solidation'.

'It's scary how much talent she has,' Gregory Mosher has said.
And to stretch her talents as a comic actress it made the most
sense for her to undertake a complete change from the depths of
seriousness of much of the *Like A Prayer* album and the dramatic
Broadway part she had played for months prior to that. Even so,
early in 1989 it was announced that she would appear in the film
Triumph, playing a victim of the Nazi holocaust in Auschwitz during
World War II, but she did not continue with that project. Shortly
afterwards, as a genuinely complete change, she accepted the part of
Breathless Mahoney, starring opposite Warren Beatty in *Dick Tracy*,
a modern version of the 1930s (and later) comic-strip detective, the
cop with the jutting jaw, pulled trilby and two-way wrist radio.

Shooting began in Hollywood in April 1989, with Stephen
Sondheim agreeing to write three songs for Madonna's 'siren'
character. Early reports suggest that her performance may well
turn out to be the most completely realized of her screen roles.

In her personal life, the divorce proceedings continue apace and
Madonna has been spotted out on the town with several 'new men'.
Some papers claim that she had an affair with Warren Beatty while
others report their constant fights on the set of *Dick Tracy*; there
were pictures of her with a mysterious, very handsome younger man,
Robert Perrino; and Madonna herself has been urging the press to
believe the rumours that she is having a lesbian relationship with
Sandra Bernhard – a trap that many have fallen into.

This friendship took a provocative new turn at the end of May
1989 when Madonna and Sandra took the stage at a charity gala,
scantily clad and dancing closely to the music. Sandra allegedly
called to the crowd, 'Believe those rumours!' Lesbianism is obviously something that certain sectors of the American public cannot,
as yet, accept with good grace. At the International Music Awards
on 1 June, Madonna easily won the year's award for Best Female
Singer but when her name was called a certain amount of cat-calling
marred the ceremony. Madonna herself did not appear.

Once again she is stirring up controversy but, like all the other
occasions, it seems certain that her fans will stay loyal and her
records continue to sell in record-breaking quantities.

CONCLUSION

What is it about Madonna that has made her, at the age of thirty-one, such a trans-continental superstar? The answer to this question is as varied and covers as wide a range of factors as the subject herself. She has reached a stage in her life when, in her own words, 'Sometimes I get this scary feeling that I could do anything I wanted.'

She has an exceptional range of creative talents and has achieved success in several different fields – as a dancer, a singer, a songwriter, a choreographer, a record producer, a 'tour' artist and an actress.

Madonna trained as a dancer. She really trained, for years, and it was her dancing skills which brought her to New York in the first place. This was no 'disco-queen', picking up a few steps at the local keep-fit class; her teachers were true professionals, some of them – Pearl Lang, especially – at the summit of their careers. To be a successful dancer, one has to have a number of skills, but the prime one has to be a sense of musical rhythm. All successful dancers are musical, and Madonna's years of dance training have contributed greatly to her success. They gave her a professional approach to choreography, and therefore the making of videos, and enabled her to dance to a high standard – when she was given the chance – as well as sing. There can be no doubt that the physical daily discipline of dance training stood her in excellent stead when touring and spending whole days working in studios, without a break until she had achieved the sound she wanted.

If, during the preceding chapters of this book, an emphasis has been placed upon the musical content of her albums, it is because it is through music that her talent first came to worldwide attention, and through her music being *heard*, not seen (although videos were made of her hits from an early stage, no-one would claim them as masterpieces of sales inducement). It was through music that we

131

first heard, and continue to hear, Madonna, and it was her music that has – against many odds, and more opinions – stood the test of time. Those who airily dismissed her as 'flavour of the month' at various points in the mid-1980s have had to eat their words, for her staying power in the notoriously transient medium of popular music has been astonishing.

She spent almost a year learning how to play drums, the piano and the guitar, adding to her musical skills, and playing in a working band, so that by the time she stood before a band as a singer she could do everything being done by any other member of the band behind her. Her training was therefore complete, but the actual timbre, the quality, of her voice was not to everyone's taste. Described by one critic as sounding like 'Minnie Mouse on helium', her voice has never been big in tone or in volume, but it has always been immediately identifiable. Within hearing one bar of a Madonna single one knew immediately who the singer was. This is a priceless attribute for a recording artist, and it is by no means as common as one might think. Indeed, one of the more remarkable aspects of Madonna's later career has been the growth of Madonna 'soundalikes', demonstrating quite clearly the potent force of her voice. What, therefore, is her voice like and why does it have this unique effect? In fact, it is a small-scale one, a voice which often sounds strained in its production, as though she were singing from the back of her throat and not from her lungs. But however it is produced, it is because of this quality that she comes across as vulnerable, threatened, completely feminine. Her voice has a greater expressiveness than might at first be supposed. In range, it is a contralto – she has no really high notes, but a surprisingly rich (in comparison) middle and lower register which adds a wordly-wise, been-around quality when called for. At the top end, her voice is clear and pure, quite able to ride over any backing tracks. And so Madonna's voice is both distinctive yet variable – qualities which any recording artist has to possess.

As a singer, Madonna soon gravitated to writing her own material and her talent as a songwriter has also to be considered. Since she knew her own voice, and she knew the importance of rhythm and syncopation from her dancing, she was able to write songs that were both distinctive and tailor-made for her abilities. Based originally on dance-styles, her songs have grown in depth and expressive seriousness so that on the one hand she is responsible for such classics as 'Into The Groove' and on the other she has created something as utterly different as 'Promise To Try'. Of course, by no means all of Madonna's songs are entirely her own work; she often writes in collaboration with others but such is her control over all aspects of the finished result that we can justly talk of 'her' material.

If her music has developed, so has her lyric-writing. Whatever the impetus for such lines, some have become phrases within most people's vocabulary; recently, on the *Like A Prayer* album her lyrics have risen to new levels of subtlety and literacy. But not all of Madonna's songs have been for herself. Such has been her consistent chart success that others have turned to her for material – either written especially for them, or (as in the case of Jellybean's house extended dance mix of 'Sidewalk Talk', with vocals by Catherine Buchanan) a new version of an existing Madonna composition.

We have chronicled her growing involvement in the technical and creative side of record production and the difficulties she experienced at first in ensuring that her ideas were realized; but for many years now Madonna has taken a leading role in these aspects of recording to the extent that she is now in demand as a record producer in her own right. This is not a career she can assume with equanimity but it is a skill she undoubtedly possesses, as the unprecedented success of the Nick Kamen single clearly shows.

As her career has developed, so have her other qualities. From a practical point of view, her videos – a mixture of her film experience and her musical creativity – have demanded a greater choreographic element, and this is something which she has always been happy to do but her choreography is always placed at the service of the music and is never flaunted for its own sake. This in turn leads to the last aspect of Madonna's performing talent, one which is best described as 'tour' artist. We must remember that Madonna achieved her first hit record without ever having performed it in public; her live appearances in New York's clubs were not succeeded by a growing acquisition of experience until she was ready to embark on her first tour. What happened was that she was catapulted directly onto the 'tour' stage, and carried the whole thing off with the confidence of someone who had been touring for years. This was an astonishing achievement, as the videos of her live performances demonstrate, and the totality of her stage presence adds the final touch to her complete and flawless armoury as a creative musician. In this regard, Madonna has certainly paid her dues.

It is by no means unknown for a pop star to be invited to appear in films, but it is unusual for a female artist to do this and to go on to exhibit an acting skill way above the normal. Madonna's film performances have not met with the universal success accorded to her records but she has demonstrated – away from popular music – a talent which embraces both comic and serious acting. In *Desperately Seeking Susan* few could remain unattracted by her characterization, and there are parts – at least – of *Who's That Girl?* which are quite beautifully played and timed. In dramatic roles, Madonna has had less acclaim but we ought not overlook *A Certain Sacrifice*, in spite of its availability only on video, nor the part of Karen in *Speed the Plough*.

Madonna, therefore, has now arrived at a high-point of her multi-faceted career. But she is undoubtedly learning a profound truth: that versatility in an artist can be a curse. If the artist has no clear perception of the future, no direct aim in life, they can be sidetracked into various projects which can dissipate their energy. Again, a multi-talented artist is not unknown, but what places Madonna on an exceptional level is the triumphant nature of her achievements. Not for her mere 'hit singles', but top three singles time after time after time.

We have seen this happen and identified the constituent parts of her artistic makeup without which this could not have happened, but the crucial question is *how* did this take place? What additional qualities does Madonna possess which ensured her success?

The first is her limitless belief in herself. All aspiring artists should have no doubt at all that they are going to succeed, and we have chronicled the setbacks and disappointments, the false starts and trails Madonna has followed in her journey to stardom – events which would have felled many a lesser man or woman. Her drive is legendary; she will not wait and can get by on very little sleep (also a characteristic of someone who eats frugally). This frees her to do more: her working day is much longer than that of most other people.

It has been claimed that Madonna used her sexual wiles to further her career. Whether or not this is true – and it has been fuelled by remarks she is reported to have made to that effect – she could hardly remain at the top of the charts for weeks on end in every country in the world which publishes a chart simply by going to bed with every man in sight. The fact also remains that Madonna's early boyfriends have all remained on good terms with her; this would hardly be the case if they had been 'used', for few men would readily admit to such a thing and would not stay friendly with the so-called 'siren'. She has been shrewd enough to work only with those with whom she gets on, but all of them are highly talented in their own right.

The loyalty she still commands and receives could not have been achieved if she did not possess one disarming quality: a good sense of humour. Madonna is fun: fun in her art, in her songs, but more importantly in her life. Her humour is the safety-valve with which she can unleash her worries and pressures.

This sense of humour is evident throughout much of her work – in her lyrics, her playful teasing sexuality and also in many of her public utterances. It is good to see her getting her own back on the journalists who used to make her life so miserable, teasing them about her relationship with Sandra Bernhard and daring them to believe that she is gay. And has anyone ever been more of a master of the double entendre? 'I got the lock baby, you got the key'; 'My box needs to be turned on'; the list is endless.

The last quality that has made Madonna so consistently success-ful throughout her career is a shrewd sense of what the public want and what they will take at any given time. She creates just enough controversy to get plenty of media attention but not so much that she loses public sympathy. She has reinvented her image several times, *á la* David Bowie, turning from the sassy, streetwise urchin to the icy femme fatale; from the crazy noisy look to a glamorous and sophis-ticated modern woman. Similarly her music has developed from the hard-edged dance hits of the early years through the soul-influenced love songs of *True Blue* to the rounded and artistically fully mature ballads of *Like A Prayer*. Some songs have shrewdly been aimed at the Hispanic and black communities, both as a compliment to the musical styles of each and, surely, as an attempt to win new fans. She may have miscalculated in some of her film projects but her music has carried her through and the variety of her work, the constant changes, have ensured that she has never become boring.

And so what is the sum total of Madonna? What has she actually achieved? By June 1989 it was estimated that in her record career of six years she had sold in excess of 85 million records. When an artist sells that many records they are very significant indeed, especially since there were no new record releases during eighteen months of those years. The result has been that she has accumulated a personal fortune estimated at around sixty million dollars and become one of the ten highest-paid entertainers of the late 1980s. As her career enters the 1990s Madonna has become possibly the most significant and sought-after female artist in the music and film professions today. This is a heavy responsibility but as time has elapsed it is clear that a simple faith and her family's support have enabled her to cope with the enormous pressure under which she now has to operate. As a child, her life and family were shattered, and there is no doubt that the death of her mother – touchingly noted in Madonna's dedication of the *Like A Prayer* album to her memory – far from destroying the little girl's self-confidence actually fuelled it, making her more determined than ever to succeed and fulfil the destiny her mother taught her was hers. In 1988 she reportedly claimed that her next move would be to have a child, but the divorce from Sean Penn will presumably make that less imminent.

Now, freed from the constraints of marriage, Madonna is at last able to choose whatever she wants to do next. At thirty-one her career is perfectly poised to achieve even greater things; she is the ultimate personification, the demonstration that it can be done, of her own advice – 'express yourself'. Given the room and opportunities in which to work, who dare say what as yet unheard, as yet unwritten, as yet unacted manifestations of Madonna's enormous talent we shall experience in the final decade of the twentieth-century, what we shall take with us as we enter the twenty-first? Only time will tell, but Madonna is already the embodiment of President Eisenhower's words, spoken seventy-two hours before her birth: 'The dream of world conformity is an impossible dream.' What her life has shown beyond all doubt is that it is perfectly possible for *non*-conformity to succeed, and to succeed triumphantly, given talent bordering on genius, a passionate belief in one's own ability, the sheer force of will, and a lucky star to make it happen.

FILMOGRAPHY

1980
A CERTAIN SACRIFICE

Running Time: approx 60 minutes
(Independent Film)
Written, Produced and Directed by Stephen Jon Lewicki
Starring: Madonna (Bruna), Jeremy Pattnosh (Dashiel)
UK Certificate: 18
Video: True Blue Productions, 1986. Catalogue number: TB 069

1984
WILD LIFE

Released: Summer 1984
Running Time: approx 92 minutes
(Universal)
Starring: Christopher Penn
Madonna single 'Burning Up' used in film as background music
to one scene
UK Certificate: 18
Video: Universal/CIC, 1984. Catalogue number VHA 1172

1984
VISION QUEST [UK TITLE: CRAZY FOR YOU]

Released: February 1985
Running Time: approx 103 minutes
(Warner Brothers)

Madonna makes a cameo appearance as a night-club singer
UK Certificate: 15
Video: Warner Brothers, 1985. Catalogue number: PEV 11459

1984
DESPERATELY SEEKING SUSAN

Released: March 1985
Running Time: approx 99 minutes
(Orion Pictures)
Executive Producer: Michael Peyser
Director of Photography: Ed Lachman
Written by: Leora Barish
Produced by: Midge Sandford and Sarah Pillsbury
Directed by: Susan Seidelman
Starring: Rosanna Arquette (Roberta), Madonna (Susan), Aidan Quinn (Jim)
UK Certificate: 15
Video: Orion/Rank Video, 1986. Catalogue number: 0235

1986
SHANGHAI SURPRISE

Released: June 1986
Running Time: approx 97 minutes
(HandMade Films)
Executive Producers: George Harrison and Denis O'Brien
Director of Photography: Ernest Vincze
Written by: John Kohn and Robert Bentley, from the novel *Faraday's Flowers* by Tony Kenrick
Produced by: John Kohn
Directed by: Jim Goddard
Starring: Sean Penn (Glendon Wasey), Madonna (Gloria Tatlock)
UK Certificate: 15
Video: [Original Version] HandMade Films/Warner Brothers, 1987. Catalogue number: PEV 11695
Second Video: [Revised Version, edited to approx 93 minutes]

HandMade Films/Warner Brothers, 1988. Catalogue number: PES 11695

1986
AT CLOSE RANGE

Released: September 1986
Running Time: approx 115 minutes
(Orion Pictures/Hemdale)
Executive Producers: John Daly, Derek Gibson
Director of Photography: Juan Ruiz Anchia
Written by: Nicholas Kazan, based upon the story by Elliott Lewitt and Nicholas Kazan
Produced by: Elliott Lewitt and Don Guest
Directed by: James Foley
Starring: Sean Penn (Brad Jr), Christopher Walken (Brad Sr)
Music by: Madonna (singing 'Live To Tell')
UK Certificate: 15
Video: Rank Video, 1987. Catalogue number: 0348

1987
WHO'S THAT GIRL?

Released: May 1987
Running Time: approx 90 minutes
(Warner Bros/Guber-Peters Company)
Executive Producers: Peter Guber, Jon Peters and Roger Birnbaum
Director of Photography: Jan DeBont
Written by: Andrew Smith and Ken Finkleman
Produced by: Rosilyn Heller and Bernard Williams
Directed by: James Foley
Starring: Madonna (Nikki Finn), Griffin Dunne (Loudon Trott)
UK Certificate: PG
Video: Warner Brothers, 1987. Catalogue number: PEV 11758

VIDEOGRAPHY
Additional to video releases of films

1985
MADONNA EP

Running Time: approx 18 minutes
(Warner Brothers)
Reference: WMV 3
Songs:
Burning Up/Borderline/Lucky Star/Like A Virgin
UK Certificate: U

1985
THE VIRGIN TOUR

Running Time: approx 50 minutes
(Warner Brothers)
Reference: 938105-3
Songs:
Dress You Up/Holiday/Into The Groove/Everybody/Gambler/
Lucky Star/Crazy for You/Over and Over/Like A Virgin/Material
Girl
Live Concert in Detroit.
Repackaged and Re-released in 1987 (same catalogue number)
UK Certificate: E

1987
IT'S THAT GIRL

Running Time: approx 60 minutes
(Sire Records)
Reference: SAM 380

Songs:
Holiday/Lucky Star/Like A Virgin/Material Girl/Into The Groove/
Angel/Dress You Up/Borderline/Live To Tell/Papa Don't Preach/
True Blue (Remix)/Open Your Heart (Remix)/La Isla Bonita
(Remix)/Who's That Girl?
Promotional Item Only: Not for Sale; a Limited Edition of 125
copies
UK Certificate: E

1988
CIAO ITALIA: LIVE FROM ITALY

Running Time: approx 100 minutes
(Warner-Reprise/Sire)
Reference: 938141-3
Songs:
Open Your Heart/Lucky Star/True Blue/Papa Don't Preach/White
Heat/Causing A Commotion/The Look of Love/Dress You Up/
Material Girl/Like A Virgin/I Can't Help Myself/Where's The
Party/Live To Tell/Into The Groove/La Isla Bonita/Who's That
Girl?/Holiday
UK Certificate: E

DISCOGRAPHY

Part 1

THE BRITISH SINGLES

1. Everybody/Everybody (dub version)
Warner Brothers W 9899
No chart position
Released December 1982
Produced by Mark Kamins
[12″ version Warner Brothers W 9899T, released December 1982]

2. Lucky Star/I Know It
Sire W 9522 (picture sleeve)
No chart position, but see also Items 4 and 18, below
Released September 1983
Produced by Reggie Lucas
[12″ version Sire W 9522T, released September 1983]

3. Holiday*/Think Of Me†
Sire W 9405 (picture sleeve)
No. 6, but see also Items 10 and 17, below
Released November 1983
Produced by John 'Jellybean' Benitez*/Reggie Lucas†
[12″ version, Sire W 9405T, released November 1983]

4. Lucky Star/I Know it
Reissue, March 1984, of item 2; identical formats and catalogue numbers
No. 14

5. Borderline/Physical Attraction
Sire W 9260 (picture sleeve)
No. 56, but see also Item 14 below
Released June 1984
Produced by Reggie Lucas
[12″ version, Sire W 9260T, released June 1984]

6. Like A Virgin/Stay
Sire W 9210 (picture sleeve)
No. 3
Released September 1984
Produced by Nile Rodgers
[12″ version, Sire W 9210T, released September 1984]

7. Material Girl/Pretender
Sire W 9083 (poster and picture sleeve versions, same catalogue number)
No. 3
Released February 1985
Produced by Nile Rodgers
[12″ version, Sire 9083T, released February 1985]

8. Crazy For You
[NB: B Side – I'll Fall In Love Again, performed by Sammy Hagar]
Geffen A 6323 (picture sleeve)
No. 2
Released June 1985
Produced by John 'Jellybean' Benitez
[Shaped picture disc, Geffen A 6323P, released June 1985]

9. Into The Groove/Shoo-Bee-Doo
Sire W 8934 (picture sleeve)
No. 1
Released July 1985
Produced by Madonna and Steve Bray
[Shaped picture disc, Sire W 8934P, released July 1985; 12″ version, including also 'Everybody', produced by Mark Kamins, Sire W 8934T, released July 1985]

10. Holiday/Think of Me
Reissue, July 1985, of Item 3; identical formats and catalogue numbers, plus 12″ picture disc Sire W 9405P, issued July 1985
No. 2

11. Angel*/Burning Up†
Sire W 8881 (picture sleeve)
No. 5
Released September 1985
Produced by Nile Rodgers*/Reggie Lucas†
[12″ version, picture sleeve, including dance mix of 'Angel', Sire W 8881T, and 12″ shaped picture disc edition, without dance mix of 'Angel', Sire W 8881P, both released September 1985]

12. The Gambler
[NB: B Side – Nature of the Beast performed by Black'n'Blue]
Geffen A 6585 (poster sleeve)
No. 4
Released October 1985
Produced by John 'Jellybean' Benitez
[7″ picture sleeve, identical catalogue number, and 12″ version, including 'The Gambler' in dance mix and instrumental only tracks, Geffen TA 6585, both released October 1985]

13. Dress You Up*/I Know It†
Sire W 8848 (picture sleeve)
No. 5
Released November 1985
[12″ versions, one with picture sleeve, the other with poster sleeve, and both including 'Dress You Up' in casual instrumental mix, released with same catalogue number Sire W 8848T, and a third 12″ version, a shaped picture disc, released with catalogue number Sire W 8848P, in November 1985]

14. Borderline/Physical Attraction
Reissue, in January 1986, of Item 5 above, with identical catalogue number for the 7″ version.
No. 2
[12″ versions, one a shaped picture disc Sire W 9260P, the other a picture sleeve but including a dub edition of 'Borderline' Sire W

9260T, released January 1986. This latter disc utilizes the same catalogue number as the initial 12″ version of Item 5, but adds the new track]

15. Live To Tell/Live To Tell (instrumental version)
Sire W 8717 (picture sleeve)
No. 2
Released April 1986
Produced by Madonna and Patrick Leonard
[12″ version, containing three editions – the two on the 7″ single, plus an extended vocal version, Sire W 8717T, released April 1986]

16. Papa Don't Preach/Ain't No Big Deal
Sire W 8636 (picture sleeve)
No. 1
Released June 1986
Produced by Madonna and Steve Bray
[12″ versions, picture sleeve Sire W 8636T, and picture disc Sire W 8636P released June 1986]

17. True Blue*/Holiday†
Sire W 8550 (picture sleeve)
No. 1
Released September 1986
Produced by Madonna and Steve Bray*/John 'Jellybean' Benitez – the track 'Holiday' is a reissue of the A side of Items 3 and 10, above.
[12″ versions, one containing 'True Blue' in the 'long version' and 'Holiday' in the LP version on Sire W 8550T, and the other a picture disc edition of the 7″ tracks on Sire W 8550P, both released September 1986]

18. Open Your Heart*/Lucky Star†
Sire W 8480 (picture sleeve)
No. 4
Released December 1986
Produced by Madonna and Patrick Leonard* (described as 'Re-mix')/Reggie Lucas†
[12″ version contains extended and dub mixes of 'Open Your Heart' and extended mix of 'Lucky Star' Sire W 8480T released December 1986]

19. La Isla Bonita/La Isla Bonita – Instrumental
Sire W 8378
No. 1
Released March 1987
Produced by Madonna and Patrick Leonard
[12″ version Sire W 8378T issued March 1987]

20. Who's That Girl?/White Heat
Sire W 8341
No. 1
Released July 1987
Produced by Madonna and Patrick Leonard
[12″ version Sire W 8341T, issued July 1987]

21. Causing A Commotion/Jimmy Jimmy
Sire W 8224
No. 4
Released September 1987
[12″ versions, one Sire 8224T, the other a picture disc edition Sire W 8224P, released September 1987]

22. The Look of Love*/I Know It†
Sire W 8115
No. 9
Released October 1987
[12″ versions, one Sire W 8115T, the other a picture disc edition Sire W 8115P, released October 1987]

23. Like a Prayer/Act of Contrition
Sire W 7539
No. 1
Released March 1989
Produced by Madonna and Patrick Leonard
[12″ versions, one Sire W 7539T containing extended remix and Club editions of 'Like a Prayer', the other a picture disc Sire W 7539P, released March 1989]

24. Express Yourself
Sire W 2948
No. 3

Released May 1989
Produced by Madonna and Stephen Bray
[12″ versions, Sire W 2948T and a picture disc edition Sire W 2948P, released May 1989]

ALBUMS

1.
MADONNA
Lucky Star/Borderline/Burning Up/I Know It/Holiday*/Think Of Me/Physical Attraction/Everybody**
Produced by Reggie Lucas/John 'Jellybean' Benitez*/Mark Kamins**
No. 1
Released September 1983
Catalogue Number: Sire 92 3867 – 1 (LP) – 4 (Cassette)
Reissued September 1985, repackaged as THE FIRST ALBUM
Catalogue Number: WX 22

A NOTE ON THE CATALOGUE NUMBERS

As has been noted in the main body of the book, Sire Records are distributed throughout the world by Warner Brothers, and are consequently obliged to use the Warner Brothers numbering system.

The Standard European numbering system for record releases, which applies to most major record companies, is to have a catalogue number which identifies the title, followed by a number, – 1, – 2, – 3, – 4, which identifies the format. Thus, – 1 indicates a 12″ 33 1/3 rpm vinyl LP; – 2 indicates the Compact Disc equivalent, – 3 indicates the Video equivalent and – 4 indicates the Cassette equivalent. This is the European system Warner Brothers adopt, but certain countries within Europe can add a catalogue number of their own for ease of reference, or stock control, or for dealer ordering, which applies only to their territory.

With this dual system, therefore, it is not unusual for an album to carry two catalogue numbers (and sometimes more, if those for other territories are to be included).

The original catalogue number for MADONNA (Madonna's first album) was 92 3867 – 1 (as shown above); when it was reissued as

MADONNA – THE FIRST ALBUM two years later, it was given the local number of WX 22. But the Compact Disc and Cassette versions of this reissued album remain with the original European Catalogue number, plus the suffixes to identify the relevant formats. This means that the Compact Disc catalogue number for THE FIRST ALBUM is 92 3867 – 2, and for the Cassette 92 3867 – 4.

2.
LIKE A VIRGIN (first release)
Material Girl/Angel/Like A Virgin/Over and Over/Love Don't Live Here Anymore/Dress You Up/Shoo-Bee-Doo/Pretender/Stay
Produced by Nile Rodgers
No. 1
Released November 1984
Catalogue Number: Sire 925 157 – 1 (LP) – 4 (Cassette)

LIKE A VIRGIN (reissue)
Material Girl/Angel/Like A Virgin/Over and Over/Love Don't Live Here Anymore/Into The Groove*/Dress You Up/Shoo-Bee-Doo/Pretender/Stay
Produced by Nile Rodgers/Madonna and Steve Bray*
No. 1
Released September 1985
Catalogue Number: Sire WX 20 (LP); 925 181 – 1 (LP); – 2 (Compact Disc); – 4 (Cassette); WX 20P (Picture Disc LP)

3.
TRUE BLUE
Papa Don't Preach/Open Your Heart/White Heat/Live To Tell/Where's The Party?/True Blue/La Isla Bonita/Jimmy Jimmy/Love Makes The World Go Round
Produced by Madonna, Patrick Leonard and Stephen Bray
No. 1
Released July 1986
Catalogue Number: Sire UK WX 54 (LP), WX 54C (Cassette); 925 442 – 1 (LP); – 2 (Compact Disc); – 4 (Cassette). Stock of WX 54 was also pressed on blue vinyl.

4.
WHO'S THAT GIRL?
Original Sound Track Recording

Songs performed by Madonna:
Who's That Girl?*/Causing A Commotion†/The Look Of Love*/
Can't Stop†
Produced by Madonna and Patrick Leonard*/Madonna and
Stephen Bray†
[The Album includes tracks performed by Duncan Fauré, Club
Nouveau, Michael Aitken, Scritti Politti and Coati Mundi]
No. 1
Released July 1987
Catalogue Number: WX 102 (LP); 925 611 – 1 (LP); – 2 (Compact
Disc); – 4 (Cassette)

5.
YOU CAN DANCE
'All songs are in a continuous sequence with the exception of the
dub versions'
Side 1:
Spotlight* / Holiday** / Everybody*** / Physical Attraction**** /
Spotlight [Dub Version]"/Holiday [Dub Version]
Produced by Stephen Bray*/John 'Jellybean' Benitez**/Mark
Kamins***/Reggie Lucas****
Additional Production and Remix by John 'Jellybean' Benitez*/
Bruce Forest and Frank Heller***
Side 2:
Over and Over*/Into The Groove**/Where's The Party?***/Over
and Over [Dub Version]"/Into The Groove [Dub Version]
Produced by Nile Rodgers*/Madonna and Stephen Bray**/
Madonna, Patrick Leonard and Stephen Bray***
Additional Production and Remix by Steve Thompson and Michael
Barbiero*/ Shep Pettibone** ***
"Available Only on the Cassette Format
Catalogue Number: WX 76 C (Cassette); 925 535 – 2 (Compact
Disc); – 4 (Cassette)
No. 8
Released November 1987

6.
LIKE A PRAYER
Like A Prayer/Express Yourself*/Love Song**/Till Death Us

Do Part/Promise To Try/Cherish/Dear Jessie/Oh Father/Keep It Together*/Spanish Eyes/Act of Contrition
Produced by Madonna and Patrick Leonard/Madonna and Stephen Bray*/Madonna and Prince**
No. 1
Released March 1989
Catalogue Number: Sire WX 238 (LP); 925 844 – 1 (LP); – 2 (Compact Disc); – 4 (Cassette)

7.
WOTUPSKI!?!
By John 'Jellybean' Benitez
Side 1, Track 2:
Sidewalk Talk
Madonna and Jellybean
Produced by John 'Jellybean' Benitez
Released May 1984
Catalogue Number: EMI (America) MLP 19011 (LP)

8.
REVENGE OF THE KILLER B's VOL 2
Side 2, Track 5:
Ain't No Big Deal
Madonna
Produced by Reggie Lucas
Released October 1984
Catalogue Number: Warner Brothers (USA) 1-25068 (LP)

9.
VISION QUEST
Original Sound Track Recording
Songs Performed by Madonna:
Side 1, Track 4 – Gambler
Side 2, Track 5 – Crazy For You
Produced by John 'Jellybean' Benitez
Released February 1985
Catalogue Number: Geffen GHS 24063 (LP)

10.
MADONNA – INTERVIEW 1
Interviews with Madonna

Baktabak Talking Pictures BAK 2042 (LP)
Picture Disc, Limited Edition
ND

11.
MADONNA – INTERVIEW 2
Interviews with Madonna
Baktabak Talking Pictures Bak 2104 (LP)
Picture Disc, Limited Edition
ND

NB: Symbols indicate the respective producers of each track.

ACKNOWLEDGEMENTS

This book could not have been written without the co-operation of a number of people, to whom thanks should be extended. They include Joanne Walker, Gill Paul of Sidgwick and Jackson, Nigel Lea-Jones, Mickey Berresheim, Frank Rodgers, Mike Fletcher, Terry Powell, George Lukan, Modwenna Chamberlain and her staff, the Offices of Seymour Stein of Sire Records, Tim Hollier, Chris Charlesworth, the Office of the Mayor of the City of Detroit, Michigan, and Brian Shingles.

Thanks should also go to those who gave permission for the quoting of copyright material, and especially to those associates of Madonna who kindly confirmed – or disowned – sayings previously attributed to them.

It would be invidious to mention them all for the comments in the book which have not been acknowledged in the text are entirely mine, and no blame should be attached to those people for opinions expressed with which the reader might disagree. These sources are sometimes acknowledged, but not always so, as it has been felt on occasion more discreet to allow such comments to remain anonymous – as indeed has been the wish of the majority of those consulted.

Finally I must thank my wife for her loving patience and forebearance during the writing of this book.

RM-W.
July 1989